Autism Spectrum Disorder and De-escalation Strategies

of related interest

No Fighting, No Biting, No Screaming
How to Make Behaving Positively Possible for People with
Autism and Other Developmental Disabilities
Bo Hejlskov Elvén
ISBN 978 1 84905 126 2
eISBN 978 0 85700 322 5

Asperger's Syndrome: That Explains Everything
Strategies for Education, Life and Just About Everything Else
Stephen Bradshaw
Foreword by Francesca Happé
ISBN 978 1 84905 351 8
eISBN 978 0 85700 702 5

**Practical Behaviour Management Solutions
for Children and Teens with Autism**
The 5P Approach
Linda Miller
ISBN 978 1 84905 038 8
eISBN 978 0 85700 184 9

**Achieving Best Behavior for Children
with Developmental Disabilities**
A Step-By-Step Workbook for Parents and Carers
Pamela Lewis
ISBN 978 1 84310 809 2
eISBN 978 1 84642 458 8

People with Autism Behaving Badly
Helping People with ASD Move On
from Behavioral and Emotional Challenges
John Clements
ISBN 978 1 84310 765 1
eISBN 978 1 84642 087 0

Autism Spectrum Disorder and De-escalation Strategies

A practical guide to positive behavioural interventions for children and young people

STEVE BROWN

Jessica Kingsley *Publishers*
London and Philadelphia

Illustrations by David Hare; reproduced with permission. Quotations by Temple Grandin on pages 24, 94, 108 and 175 are reproduced with kind permission of the Autism Research Institute. The Visual Strategies in Chapter 5 are provided with kind permission of Andrea Moore. The Risk Assessment example in the Appendix (pages 182–4) is reproduced with kind permission of Bernard Allen.

First published in 2015
by Jessica Kingsley Publishers
73 Collier Street
London N1 9BE, UK
and
400 Market Street, Suite 400
Philadelphia, PA 19106, USA

www.jkp.com

Library of Congress Cataloging in Publication Data
Brown, Steve, 1970-
  Autism spectrum disorder and de-escalation strategies : a practical guide to positive behavioural interventions for children and young people / Steve Brown.
     pages cm
  Includes index.
  ISBN 978-1-84905-503-1
  1. Children with autism spectrum disorders. 2. Children with autism spectrum disorders--Education. 3.
  Behavior therapy--Methods. I. Title.
   RJ506.A9B77 2015
   618.92'85882--dc23
                                    2014023054

British Library Cataloguing in Publication Data
A CIP catalogue record for this book is available from the British Library

ISBN 978 1 84905 503 1
eISBN 978 0 85700 909 8

Printed and bound in Great Britain

*I dedicate this book to my beautiful family and inspiration:
Andrea, Zac, Alex, Sam and Luke*

*In memory of Neil Roberts (1959–2013) and
Mick Atter (1951–2014)*

ACKNOWLEDGEMENTS

This book would not have happened without the help, support and encouragement of the following people to whom I am grateful: Andrea Moore (for de-escalating *my* behaviour whilst I was writing, and also for giving her kind permission to use the Visual Strategies), Chris Collette, George Matthews, Ross Weppler, Bernard Allen (for giving his kind permission to use the Risk Assessment) and Dave Hare (for the wonderful illustrations), and Jessica Kingsley Publishers. I thank Andrea Moore, Craig Keenan and Trish Miles for their outstanding proofreading and guidance. I also thank my parents, Lee, Caroline, Aunty Evelyn, Brenda Moore, Craig (Dez) and Chris Wood for their friendship, warmth and understanding.

CONTENTS

Introduction

Knowledge and timber shouldn't be much used until they are seasoned.
– Oliver Wendell Holmes, Sr.

'Education, Education, Education!' screamed the then UK prime minister after the 1997 general election. I think it would have been better to have said, 'Behaviour, Behaviour, Behaviour!' Most, if not all, staff who care for or educate children of any age have difficulties with managing children's behaviour at some point in their working life. Some staff continually face the prospect of having to manage and modify children's behaviour throughout their careers. I know, because I'm one of them. The world over, children with autism spectrum disorder (ASD) can cause adults headaches, frustration, bewilderment and upset in a range of settings.

I have worked in various settings from special schools with profound and multiple learning difficulties, severe learning difficulties and moderate learning difficulties to mainstream primary and secondary schools. I have visited and supported children on remand and have been part of an autism outreach team in one of the largest local authorities in the UK. I have discovered what can work and how to use strategies and interventions to meet the requirements of both adults and children. It is important to acknowledge that not all interventions work all of the time with every child, but it is right to presume that 99.9 per cent of children's behaviour can be managed through a vast range of ideas and interventions that adults must persevere with until they have exhausted every angle and possibility. Children with special educational needs can appear to have many letters after their name illustrating their diagnosis. (It can read like an honours list!) One such diagnosis is called Emotional Behaviour Difficulties (EBD). Sometimes my take on it is that some children are 'EBD' ('every bloody day') – children who have great character and can drive me to the edge because of behaviours that can challenge me. They are often the best children to support because they have fantastic personalities and I can see the potential that would be lost if I, alongside other people, did not try to support them. Children across the autistic spectrum have amazing abilities, and it is a crime for these children not to be supported to achieve in life. By the way, my take on EBD is not an official diagnosis!

Regarding managing children's behaviour and de-escalating difficult situations, I haven't always succeeded and I am not afraid to experience and share my own sense of failure. I can only think of a few occasions when I have thought that I personally failed a child, and that was because I wasn't skilled or experienced enough to help at that time or that a lack of time had been the problem, especially when working within a busy outreach team with a large caseload. I have sometimes made mistakes and my decisions have been wrong, but I have gained the necessary knowledge and skills to try not to make them again.

De-escalation is difficult to define. It could be defined as reducing the level of intensity of a conflict. When faced with behaviours that are challenging or unsafe, we aim to take measures to attempt to de-escalate conflict and avoid confrontation.

This book has several aims:

- to give information, advice and practical interventions to enable staff in a range of settings to improve their de-escalation skills and challenge a child's behaviour by acting in the child's best interests

- to explore the important issue of how adults manage their own feelings and how they read children's feelings through their communication

- to discuss the merits of how physical interventions and positive handling techniques can help keep children and adults safe.

This book is a practical guide on how children's behaviour and their feelings can be challenged, influenced and modified. This book has been created as a very concise, practical guide for busy staff or parents. In my experience behaviour is rarely academic and in need of vast psychological analysis, although this can be found in certain examples. In fact, inappropriate, disruptive and unsafe behaviour is a block to academic success and to a child realising their potential to be happy and succeed. It is very difficult to remove certain behaviours altogether so that they never appear again. Once a particular behaviour has been learnt, it tends to stay in the child's memory and armoury.

Children challenge us through their behaviour. This challenging behaviour can prompt reactions from adults. Alternatively, this can be viewed as behaviours that challenge us. Either way I view these behaviours as a difficult and demanding task to be modified and altered in the best interests of the child or young person. The challenge is to maintain a consistent approach that teaches a different way so that the child can learn more appropriate responses.

The interventions and strategies in this book are based on positive outcomes for the child and adult. Sometimes it is necessary for the strategy to be allowed enough time to do its work. This is often the problem when staff give up on the idea and intervention too early because they do not see instant results. I would allow at least 2 weeks for a strategy to embed before reviewing the effectiveness, although of course we will have exceptions to the rule: some children on the spectrum rely on an intervention, such as a visual timetable, all through their school days; others need several interventions at the same time or for shorter periods of time.

Physical interventions, including restraint, have been a contentious issue for a very long time (too long, in fact). Physical interventions frequently go hand in hand with non-physical strategies. This book explores this theory and looks at the legalities that allow staff to make risk assessments to try to keep children and others as safe as possible.

De-escalation and behaviour management skills are two categories that attract a lot of attention and are in high demand. De-escalating behaviour day in and day out is usually exhausting and extremely hard work. Simple solutions tend to get forgotten, and chaos, confusion and lack of confidence sometimes take over and exacerbate the problems. There will always be more than one way of de-escalating behaviour that presents as challenging, unsafe, attention seeking or disruptive. The trick, if there is one, is to match the interventions to the behaviour, and in the autism world we need to evaluate how the level of communication and understanding contributes to the challenges and then respond positively, assertively and confidently.

CHAPTER 1

Autism Spectrum Disorder and Behaviour

My apologies to those of you who have already read about autism spectrum disorder (ASD) as a condition. This chapter will be a refresher for some readers and will provide new, valuable information for others. The de-escalation, communication and behaviour management ideas I mention and explain in this book relate primarily to children and young people with ASD. I currently support and work with staff who face the task of working in establishments that support children with emotional, social and behavioural difficulties as well as children with ASD. I think that any strategy used for supporting a child on the spectrum is equally useful for helping another child who has a different diagnosis.

I have a begrudging respect for the condition of ASD, as it does not discriminate. It does not matter what the colour of your skin is, if you are rich or poor, where you live in the world or what your level of intelligence is. I cannot think of many things in life that do not discriminate in these ways.

ASD is a complex condition that affects children and adults in various ways. I often hear from people who know ASD inside out that no two individuals are the same. I think that is true and certainly remarkable. Any child with ASD that you may come into contact with will need a slightly different approach. The downside to this is that staff can become exhausted trying to mix and match the appropriate interventions for each child. I also think that all children are different anyway because of their personality, background and experiences. There is something about the autistic mind that very much individualises behaviour and communication in more dimensions than in a child without ASD. To complicate matters further, many children who have been diagnosed with ASD have an additional diagnosis (e.g. attention deficit hyperactivity disorder, Tourette syndrome or obsessive–compulsive disorder). When this occurs, it can be frustrating and immensely difficult to manage behaviours that are shooting from all directions.

Children with ASD often find the world very challenging. This in turn may lead to adults feeling challenged. Each child will have behaviours that might challenge us. Some we can ignore, while others will drive us to despair (the child probably feels the same way about the adults!). The adult needs to have enough empathy to acknowledge the fact that some behaviours will be very challenging to them. I feel that this means appreciating the child's perception of the world. I guess it boils down to seeing where the other person is coming from. This might be achieved by using a different 'lens' to view their behaviour through – the 'autism lens'.

There is no blood test or one certain feature to determine if a child is on the spectrum. Normally in the UK children are referred to a health professional when there are concerns regarding their level of communication and/or if they have problems with their behaviour. Staff in settings often use words like odd, bizarre, strange, inappropriate or dangerous to describe the child's behaviour. These expressions may not be kind or even thoughtful in the context they are given. This is why I feel very strongly that it is important to investigate a possible diagnosis for children who are displaying ASD traits. If society is to hand them a label, then for the sake of that child he or she needs to receive the correct one. ASD is unfortunately a lifelong condition, but with adult intervention children can improve their quality of life and access aspects of work and life that children without ASD can achieve. Over the years there has been a great deal of time and money spent on researching the causes of ASD. Pellicano *et al.* (2013) found that the US spends 89 times more on autism research than the UK. They go on to say that although research hasn't yet identified a genetic or biological signature, ASD is a highly genetic condition. Diagnosis is usually made by medical professionals. It is easy for professionals in settings to unofficially diagnose children by using their own level of experience and expertise. Here is a word of warning when talking to other professionals, and especially to parents: if you are not qualified to diagnose, be very careful with how the information is presented. The family of the child needs to be treated with the utmost respect when relaying concerns, and staff need to share their assessments, observations and feelings with sensitivity. It is better to describe traits and behaviours through checklists and observations when sharing concerns.

For the past 16 years I have been trying to become as skilled and knowledgeable as possible when supporting children with ASD, and certain aspects of this knowledge get challenged. The majority of the children I have supported over the years have been male, and this has led me to believe that ASD appeared to be more prevalent in males. Presently, I am not so convinced. I think lots of girls have been missed over the years. During my final few years working in an autism outreach team I noticed the referral rates for girls had increased significantly. I am not sure why. The ratio is still more in favour of boys, and it will become increasingly interesting to see in the next ten years if the gap closes between the number of boys diagnosed in relation to girls. The National Autistic Society's Lorna Wing Centre has also seen an increase in the number of referrals of young women. The referrals often come through mental health services, as the symptoms were missed during childhood.

Differences in sensory processing, social communication, social interaction and social imagination usually become noticeable as a baby or in early childhood (generally before the age of 5 years). The *Diagnostic and Statistical Manual of Mental Disorders* (DSM-5 2013) suggests that the symptoms may not manifest until 'social demands exceed limited capacities' (p.50). This could explain why behaviours seem to occur during big transitions such as starting nursery or school. Intelligence often does not come into play and the profile is often uneven. I supported a child who at age 3.5 years could not communicate socially but told his nursery teacher how many sides a hexagon had and what the angles were. The rest of the children were still talking about squares and triangles. Another child who could not talk and was unable to dress himself was able to complete a 100-piece jigsaw puzzle face down.

ASD is complex and confusing and worth getting to know. Below are a few points of note in each of the areas mentioned.

Social communication

Here are some complications related to social communication:

- Many children have difficulty understanding the purpose of communication.

- Sometimes people do not develop meaningful speech.

- There may be a processing delay.

- Echolalia (the automatic repetition of another person's speech) is common.

- Many children have difficulty interpreting language beyond the literal.

My top-six literal misunderstandings are:

1. Could you turn the light on? (The child thinks, *Yes, but I am not going to turn it on.*)

2. Paint the child next to you. (The child goes home with a blue face.)

3. Take your book out. (The child takes the book out of the room.)

4. Get your skates on! (The child says or thinks, *I haven't got any skates.*)

5. Sandwiches line up at the door. (The child thinks, *No! I am not a sandwich.*)

6. Watch the board while I go through it. (Luke Jackson, a young person with autism who wrote *Freaks, Geeks and Asperger Syndrome*, thought he was about to see a magic trick during a maths lesson and was very disappointed!)

Literal understanding can cause embarrassment, and children sometimes react inappropriately when they feel humiliated. They may overreact because they don't want people to know they have misunderstood. Not understanding jokes can make them feel more socially isolated too. They may rely on physical interaction and slapstick humour, which many young people outgrow in teenage years. An 11-year-old boy was visibly becoming aggressive when peers laughed because he had misunderstood an instruction. I took responsibility for the error by explaining to the class that it was my fault and that I hadn't explained it properly. This immediately diffused the situation and he calmed down. I later took him to one side to explain the meaning of the comment.

Social understanding

The complications below are related to social understanding:

- The child may be socially isolated; sometimes this is an issue, other times the child prefers it this way.

- The social demands of others can cause anxiety such as not knowing what to say during social 'chit-chat'.

- Social cues may be difficult to read such as knowing when to stop talking or join a conversation.

- Often behaviour is socially inappropriate such as making personal comments or picking one's nose in public.

- Friendships may be wanted, but the strategies to establish and maintain them are often lacking.

- The child may have difficulties with empathy or how to respond when someone is upset or angry.

- Interactions are often one-sided (i.e. talking 'at' people).

- Eye contact is frequently inappropriate – too much, too little or none at all.

- Attachments can be to adults or objects rather than to peers.

- The child may struggle with making sense of social rules, which may appear confusing and difficult to understand.

- The child may be vulnerable to being bullied or 'picked on'. In 2012 an American study (Anderson 2012) found that 63 per cent of children with autism had been bullied In the UK, the Anti-Bullying Alliance reported that in 2012 the number of children with autism who stated they had been bullied in school ranged from 40–82 per cent (Anti-Bullying Alliance 2013).

Social imagination

Social imagination may involve the following issues:

- Imaginative play can be lacking or the line between fantasy and reality gets blurred.

- Predicting how other people think and feel can be a challenge.

- The world can seem to be an unpredictable place which can cause anxiety or withdrawal.

- Anxiety and insecurity are common feelings.

- Many children have difficulty understanding that other people have their own ideas.

- Obsessive and ritualistic behaviour can occur.

- Many children have difficulty generalising skills or ideas from one context to another.

In a special school, a child used to dictate how everything needed to be done in a classroom and always wanted things done in a certain way or he would hit at adults until he was satisfied that it was how he wanted things done. We built in small changes to challenge his control, such as taking slightly different routes on excursions, and changed things on his timetable. Yes, we got hit a few times in the process, but he became more able to manage change and let others have some control.

One teenage boy regularly manipulated, controlled and bullied his parents and younger brother. He deliberately tried to cause his parents to separate and tried to kill his brother because he wanted to watch something else on TV. Control was regained subtly by manipulating situations where he had to adhere to other people's agendas. As a stickler for time keeping, I deliberately kept him waiting to illustrate that he was not in control. Information was shared with key people and his bullying was exposed. He was placed in a position where he had to acknowledge what he had been trying to do. His control had been dismantled to a point where he was no longer a threat to others.

Sensory sensitivities

> *I hated writing with pencils because I can actually feel the lead scraping across the paper and it makes me shudder. The sound makes me shiver so I put my fingers in my ears.*
>
> – Joshua West, aged 13

David Mitchell comments how sensory information is unfiltered and therefore overwhelming. He highlights how fabric freshener in clothes can smell as strong as air freshener being fired up your nostrils (Mitchell and Higashida 2013).

Some children have sensory differences with the five main senses and also with balance (vestibular) and body awareness (proprioception). Children can be either hyposensitive or hypersensitive to their surroundings. When children are hyposensitive, they often seek the feedback they crave (e.g. feel the need to be held very tightly). The opposite happens for children who may be hypersensitive, where they avoid certain situations (e.g. traffic noise or bright lights).

With regard to the five main senses, hyper- and hyposensitivity can be described as follows:

Sight

- *Hypersensitivity.* The child may find colours, patterns and flashing lights distressing. They may focus on particular detail and be easily distracted visually.

- *Hyposensitivity.* The child may flap hands in front of their face. They may concentrate on peripheral vision and have poor depth perception and problems with grasping things (e.g. catching balls).

Behavioural concerns are often due to distractibility and lack of attention or concentration.

Hearing

- *Hypersensitivity.* The child often covers their ears and makes their own noises to drown out noise they can't control. They have difficulty concentrating and may be able to hear distant sounds better than close sounds.

- *Hyposensitivity.* The child makes their own noises. They may ignore certain sounds but tune into others and probably enjoy noisy places.

Behaviour issues are often linked to the child making noises and distracting others or refusing to go into assembly. They may struggle in busy classrooms and withdraw under tables or leave without permission.

Smell

- *Hypersensitivity.* The child dislikes areas such as bathrooms, kitchens and dining rooms. They also dislike body smells, certain perfumes or deodorants and so forth.

- *Hyposensitivity.* The child may lick and sniff objects and people as well as seek strong odours.

Children may display challenging behaviours to avoid going into rooms or may smear (e.g. faeces or saliva).

Taste

- *Hypersensitivity.* The child is a fussy eater. They prefer bland food and feel that certain textures can cause discomfort.

- *Hyposensitivity.* The child may eat inappropriate objects and materials. They prefer strong or odd flavours.

The eating of inappropriate items can cause concerns for staff and require extra supervision.

Touch

- *Hypersensitivity.* The child does not like to touch things or to be touched, even lightly (tactile defensive). They are more likely to be resistant to physical contact. They may be unable to touch certain substances or clothes and show resistance to hair and teeth brushing. If a child is hypersensitive to touch, there will be a problem playing team sports.

- *Hyposensitivity.* The child may need to touch people, objects and materials. They may sometimes engage in self-harming. They are likely to have a high pain threshold and enjoy pressure (tight clothes and hugs).

Issues often arise from children either touching others or refusing to wear certain clothes such as school uniforms. Often young children undress and this obviously causes issues in preschool.

Balance

With regard to balance (vestibular), hyper- and hyposensitivity can be described as follows:

- *Hypersensitivity.* The child probably dislikes and/or fears heights. They cannot tolerate change in head position and become dizzy and sick easily. Car journeys can be difficult.

- *Hyposensitivity.* The child craves movement (e.g. climbing and jumping) and has difficulty sitting still. They would probably enjoy fairground rides.

Behavioural concerns are often linked to excess movement which distracts others and themselves.

Body awareness

Body awareness (proprioception) includes gauging the force needed to do activities, the sense of body position and receiving information from receptors in muscles. Examples of ASD behaviours include rocking, spinning and flapping.

Children may be unaware of personal space and have difficulty in judging distances and bump into objects and people. This may give the impression of being clumsy. They may have low muscle tone and be floppy or stumble. Difficulties often occur with fine motor skills such as tying shoe laces, doing buttons and handwriting.

Often behaviours arise from children perhaps playing too roughly, hugging too tightly or pushing too hard, as they may not realise how much force they are using.

Following the death of a close family member, a child's behaviour became more extreme requiring two-person holds on a regular basis. At first we thought it was an angry reaction to his bereavement; however, when there was a changeover during holds he waited for staff to swap places before resisting. It became clear that the child was seeking the deep-pressure experience which he gained from the restrictive holds. He wanted physical contact and we just told him to ask for a hug if he needed or wanted it, instead of being aggressive. This worked with immediate effect. Due to his autism, he had not considered asking for a hug.

Executive function

Executive function is about how people monitor and control their thoughts and actions. It includes working memory, planning and cognitive flexibility. Difficulties can be seen with the following:

- impulse control and self-regulation

- engaging and disengaging attention

- switching tasks (i.e. perseveration)

- generating novel responses

- working memory

- flexibility of thinking (may partake in rigid, repetitive behaviour)

- managing change (have a preference for the known).

Many children with ASD find it difficult to switch tasks and understand the process of start and finish. When there is a lack of organisational skills and memory retention, this usually leads to confusion and frustration. Children with attention deficit hyperactivity disorder (ADHD) also often have executive function difficulties.

Central coherence

Central coherence was described by Kanner as an inability to experience wholes without giving full attention to the constituent parts. Children may have difficulty understanding the gist of something or 'miss the point'. The weak central coherence theory was proposed by Frith in 1989. Implications of weak central coherence in children are as follows:

- difficulty choosing and/or prioritising

- difficulty organising

- difficulty generalising

- having their own preferences prominent in tasks

- may have a good rote memory

- may have comprehension difficulties despite good reading accuracy.

It is amazing how children with ASD can 'home in' on the details of a task or situation that the majority of other people can dismiss as irrelevant. I have observed children in classrooms where they have sat through a lesson and then asked a question that is reasonable but also immaterial. They may also switch their attention to a special interest that is prompted by a conversation and go off on a tangent. Staff often are driven to distraction when I visit children in various settings when they comment, 'He could do the work yesterday' or 'She is just refusing to follow instructions, this wasn't a problem before'. It is important to appreciate that many children do not automatically transfer skills from one context to another.

I am unable to hold one piece of information in my mind while I do the next step.

– Temple Grandin (2006)

These are a handful of examples of behaviours that children with ASD exhibit. Hopefully these examples will shed light on why children with ASD react the way they do to the world around them. Behaviours are often driven by feelings and thoughts. Anxiety impacts how children with ASD cope with social situations. Imagine a moment in your social life where you were invited to a party but you did not know anyone except the person with whom you were going. Think how it feels in that moment when you first enter the room and people you have never met approach you and introduce themselves, and the confusion this often entails. Later, when the person you came with is occupied with other guests and you are left on your own, comes that feeling of awkwardness and trying not to appear foolish or clumsy in front of others. This is how many children on the spectrum feel when they are trying to blend into their school, family or society.

Any person can react to a situation and display certain behaviours that will be challenging to those around them. When a child has a diagnosis of ASD and they have difficulties as described above, it is not too difficult to understand why we need to apply specific interventions. Neither is it problematic to consider why adults need to manage their non-verbal communication and the language that conveys requests, instructions and information.

◇◇◇

KEY POINTS

- Children are diagnosed with ASD by observing and assessing behaviour, including their ability to think, communicate and socialise.

- Match the strategies with the child's behaviour. Consider the child's language development as a key area to support.

- Keep updating your knowledge about ASD.

◇◇◇

CHAPTER 2

De-escalation

The average person looks without seeing, listens without hearing, touches without feeling, moves without physical awareness, inhales without awareness of odour or fragrance, and talks without thinking.

— Leonardo da Vinci

What is de-escalation?

I once planned 2 hours delivery of de-escalation strategies on a training course when, after 1.5 hours, a course member approached me and said very politely, 'I need to leave early if that's okay – I was wondering when you were going to do the de-escalation part...' To say my shoulders slumped would be an understatement. I really wanted to say, 'What do you think I've been hammering on about all this time?'

It's an easy assumption to make. De-escalation is more often than not subtle, good child management. When staff de-escalate well, it is almost like the child doesn't realise it, and if they do, it is too late anyway because by then they are already calmer and more cooperative. De-escalation is generally about acting. When a child is presenting challenging behaviours and an unfavourable attitude, it is worth remembering that it is acceptable to pretend and communicate positively even when we don't want to or don't feel like doing this. I would describe it like falling into a hole and having to think of ways to climb out. Children place adults in difficult positions time and time again. In my own practice I become 'all de-escalated out' sometimes. It is tiring and hard work; however, it is always important that I do de-escalate in the right manner and in the best interests of the child.

It is of course different with every child and how their autism spectrum disorder (ASD) affects their behaviour. If you know the child, it can give you a head start and that is often enough to get you through the process. If it is a child you don't know very well, or this happens to be the first meeting, then it is about sticking to the basics and doing them well. De-escalation requires versatility. Perhaps what makes de-escalation confusing to staff is that they are not always sure of their best approach. Confidence plays its part in all of this. As a trainer delivering courses on de-escalation and positive handling, my number one goal is to improve the confidence of course members. When presenting on Team Teach courses I want the course members to become more confident in their approach. I feel that once they see how simply de-escalation strategies can be implemented, they can start to practise and think about previous incidents and learn from mistakes and experiences.

It is not the mountain we conquer but ourselves.

– Sir Edmund Hilary

I often joke that I have four children and a dog, and that I might as well have five children or five dogs because they have two things in common: both dogs and children need adult guidance and can smell fear; also, my dog and children rarely ever follow a request first time of asking!

If children see how the adult gets uptight and wound up, they will do the behaviour more or start playing games just to reinforce that they have got the better of the adult. It's all about doing the opposite and protecting yourself from being wound up and compromised. My brother has a tactic he implements skillfully when dealing with difficult situations that people have created: do the opposite of what they are expecting. I feel that an escalating situation is usually 10 per cent of how the child behaves and communicates and 90 per cent of how the adult reacts. The adult is in the more difficult position because we have the 90 per cent with which to concern ourselves; we have to be the consistent role model and react in a reasonable and proportionate manner. The adult is also very often the person who walks away frazzled and exhausted after de-escalating a situation.

The child is ordinarily the person who quickly forgets what's happened and then moves on to something else. Nobody ever said de-escalation is easy!

The reality is that de-escalation strategies need to be simple, robust and consistent. I often witness staff over-complicate issues and situations that then escalate a child's behaviour and it becomes open warfare, a massive power struggle or a win/lose situation.

Just before the fall of Saigon during the Vietnam War, an American general commented to a Vietnamese officer nearby, 'We never lost a major battle during this war.' The Vietnamese replied, 'That is irrelevant, is it not?' This exchange must have been repeated over the history of time and has become a military oxymoron. Think back to Hannibal attacking the Romans in 216 BC and Sparta vs Athens. Both won every battle they fought but still ended up on the losing side. This leads to the old saying 'Pick and choose your battles, because you can win every battle and still lose the war'. As the adult we might feel it a necessity to come out on top of the situation every time, but is this the way to build up trust, role-model-appropriate behaviour and improve relationships?

> *Unacceptable behaviour is part of the human condition.*
> – Clements and Zarkowska (2000)

This statement is a fact for us all to contemplate. Have you ever witnessed educational professionals on a staff night out? Never mind that, what about staff on a training day? All the behaviours that staff moan and complain about – they participate in the same things! During some courses I deliver on de-escalation and physical intervention I have to remind course members before lunch that they should only take a limited amount of food and then come back for more once everyone has had their first share. These are adults and they have to be managed like children! A lot of the course members cannot concentrate for more than 30 minutes even when given opportunities to discuss and ask questions, watch video clips or enter a debate. Yet children are expected to attend a provision for at least 6 hours per day, 5 times a week, and follow all staff instructions and requests first time and not cause any problems.

In my adopted hometown of Birmingham, England, there are often political party conferences. One particular year the politicians were given reduced entry to 'strip joints' as a perk (hardly the best environment for role-modelling acceptable behaviour). All adults who work with children of any age sometimes display unacceptable behaviour in their lives. If we can all admit this, maybe the children will be cut some slack and not have to follow rules such as:

- Always be polite.

- Always work hard.

- Be quiet.

- Always do your best.

- Always do as you are told the first time (my personal favourite).

Who makes up these impossible rules? Show me a school or care setting where all the staff actually follow these rules themselves and I will stand corrected.

As adults we need to be extremely careful about the standards we set, the rules we establish and the expectations we have. Look at where the children are starting from and acknowledge that first. Then look to move the children on to a better place. Be realistic, keep looking back and remember where they started. Let us make those reasonable adjustments that children with ASD need. Let us consider their areas of difficulties and be brave and forward-thinking enough to make allowances. Before we even consider what interventions to use or not to use, it is vitally important to be realistic. I often witness professionals fall into a trap where the child with ASD is expected to behave and respond in the same manner as a child who never causes a problem or always does the right thing. Autism spectrum disorder is a lifelong condition; there are aspects that never go away, and this needs to be understood from the very start.

How de-escalation is like playing golf

I am not a golfer. I have played once or twice and the best two balls I hit all day were when I trod on a rake. I have never exhibited a natural flair for the game, and I have seen experienced people sling their golf clubs across the fairway (never to be seen again) and then break down and cry. A person cannot play golf and master this sport without a bag full of different clubs which enable the golfer to choose the best method of hitting the ball to successfully get it to where it needs to go next. De-escalating behaviour is the same. To achieve the most successful outcome or safest approach, there needs to be a wide choice of interventions (golf clubs) from which to choose. This way, there is always a strategy to try that meets the needs of the situation. Golf balls and children are fairly similar too – both have a mind of their own and end up in places you don't want them to be! Let us discover and explore some of the de-escalation interventions that can support children on the spectrum and lots of other children too.

An important rule of golf is how many clubs you can carry around the course. Golfers are allowed a maximum of 14 clubs. These clubs are divided into categories. Staff should consider how many strategies are needed to support a child and his or her behaviour and adjust these strategies accordingly. Too many de-escalation strategies make them difficult to implement consistently, and not enough may leave us short on ideas.

De-escalation strategies
Using checklists
Staff can avoid problems by using checklists. Lots of professionals use checklists to remind them of what they need to do and what they need to remember. Airline pilots, racing car drivers, chefs, surgeons, nurses, civil litigation and electricians all use checklists to help inform them of risk and solutions in more high-risk circumstances; however, checklists should not be used to replace common sense. Sometimes we have to rely on gut instinct and overrule the checklist. For the majority of the time, using a checklist to guide us through a problem is certainly very helpful.

Here are three examples of checklists to help with children's behaviour:

Example 1

1. Recognise the problem: is there a problem?

2. Causes: make a list.

3. Options: discuss with others.

4. Solution(s): make a list.

5. Implementation: evaluate.

6. What has changed?

Example 2

1. Recognise the problem(s).

2. Ask team members for points of view.

3. Ask for opinions from outside professionals.

4. Give feedback.

5. Devise a strategy.

Example 3 (devised for staff that used a 'reflection room' for children who needed their own space)

1. Keep your distance (*stay safe*).

2. Stand sideways (*less intimidating*).

3. Listen (*don't talk too much*).

4. Tone of voice (*assertive, gentle and direct*).

5. Change of face (*ask for/accept help*).

Managing transitions

It is very important to remember how difficult transitions can be for students with ASD. These can be daily transitions from lesson to lesson (even if they don't change rooms) or larger-scale transitions such as moving class or leaving school. If transitions are prepared and planned well, behavioural difficulties are likely to be reduced or not occur in the first place. Talking to parents is really important to understand what students need. Strategies I have used for daily transitions include:

- allowing children to leave their lesson early so that they avoid the hustle and bustle of lots of people moving around school (also supports children with sensory or organisational difficulties)

- giving pupils specific jobs to do during transition times within the classroom so they can remain focused and know when their job is finished – very handy during 'tidy up time' in primary schools when 'tidy up' seems to be a free-for-all with lots of movement

- pre-tutoring for movement from one place to another such as using symbols as reminders of where they are going and how they need to move – quietly

- having a specific place in a line whilst waiting or queuing up.

Examples of strategies I have used for larger transitions include the following:

- *Photo books.* These are to prepare for day trips or residential events. Often trips are to the same place each year so group photos can be taken. Remember to include how they will get there (e.g. by coach) and what time they will get back to school.

- *Transition books.* These are made using photographs of the new environment and future staff. The children can take them home to prepare themselves for the change and discuss their worries with parents or staff. They help to reduce anxieties such as a child worrying about which toilet they will use or where they will go for dinner.

- *One-page profiles.* These are single sheets with hints and tips for staff on what a child needs and how to manage behaviours. These profiles are great for sharing with supply staff and new teachers. The children and parents can contribute as well as staff who know them well. The profiles might say something like, 'John needs time to process what you say – if you talk too fast, he overloads and gets agitated' or 'Mary gets very anxious when people she doesn't know talk to her – please try not to ask her too many questions'.

- Extra visits to new settings – first a short visit perhaps with parents or carers, then a longer visit which might include lunch – building up to the main transition day.

Staying calm

Remain calm. Be kind.

The key is not to make quick decisions, but to make timely decisions.

– General Colin L. Powell

It is vitally important that the adults try to stay calm when de-escalating the child's behaviour. Staying calm encourages the child with ASD to engage in flexible thinking. This type of thinking is essential to enable them to process and to reflect on the options and choices we give them. If the adults become panic stricken, fearful and confused (three easy emotions to experience when facing difficult behaviour), it is likely the child will experience the same emotions. They are looking for us to be consistent and composed. The main problem associated with adults when they become stressed and pressured is that the strategies become locked away somewhere we cannot quite reach but know they are there. This can happen quickly.

A tactic for staying calm and in control of our own feelings is to vocalise our thoughts. This is not to be confused with random talking that sounds like incoherent rambling. Children with ASD do not always understand how other people are feeling or thinking. Due to the nature of this condition, they are not able to predict what needs to happen next and do not understand what the adult is expecting. Vocalising our thoughts can help the child to recognise emotions and feelings and can assist with the child's sequencing of changing their behaviour. The adult can offer options or restricted choices through vocalisation. This type of communication is more non-threatening than a direct approach such as giving directives or commands. If the adult speaks in a calm, matter-of-fact voice, the child can find it easier to process the words. Autistic children cannot readily read the adult's red face, raised eyebrows and gritted teeth that indicates frustration or dissatisfaction. Visualising the options or choices helps to remind the child and encourages easier processing. This works especially well when the child is very anxious, confused and stressed. One additional advantage to using this strategy is that it assists the adult in thinking through their ideas, receiving feedback from the child and letting the other staff know what their thinking is.

Remaining confident

There have been many times during incidents or situations where a child has displayed very difficult behaviour and I have been at a loss (I never consider myself an expert) as to what to do for the best outcome. In these situations I remember a time when I found a decent answer. In 2004 my first child was born. Like many fathers I went through the 9 months of celebrating the notion of having a child, suffered alongside the child's mother and took the insults on the chin(s). 'You don't know what it's like unless you are about to pass a bowling ball!' was a personal favourite along with 'It's okay for the bloke, he's done his part, such as it is!' It's good that I can de-escalate when I need to: never mess with a pregnant woman is very sound advice – and if you do, make sure you turn sideways and get your head out of the way!

Towards the end of the birthing process, when the midwife decided to turn up after the father had been holding the fort (rather well I thought) and the medical staff (who hadn't been seen all night) decided to put in an appearance, then nudged me out of the way, it started to get to the serious business end of it all – rather like the crisis part of a child's behaviour. What is going to happen next? What I do or don't do in the next few minutes will determine the outcome. I remember looking at the midwife as she struggled to get my son out, the exhausted mother looking like an antelope that had just been chased down by a pride of lions. I started to panic. My feet were going in different directions and my mouth was moving with nothing coming out. At that point I looked over my shoulder and froze. Standing behind me were six medical professionals. I looked at each person individually and they all stood there confident in their ability to perform the next action that was necessary. There was a lady who I took to be the lead midwife who I presumed was only ever involved in the delivery process if the baby was in serious trouble. She looked towards me with a friendly determination and nodded her head slightly with a faint smile. I instantly relaxed and smiled. I had every faith this person could perform miracles and sort out any problem. This was the look I needed to perfect when faced with angry, aggressive and awkward behaviour. It was all in the body language, of course, in the facial expressions. Pure reassurance and confidence exuded from her.

My son was saved by the brilliant skill of the paediatrician who turned him in the womb to a safe position to be delivered. The midwife later told me that he was the only person in the hospital who could perform that manoeuvre. The paediatrician may have known the trick, but it was the lead midwife who calmed me down and gave the reassurance I needed to stay in control of my emotions, which was achieved purely through her non-verbal communication. If those staff at the back of the room had not oozed confidence and looked like they knew what they needed to do next, I would have continued to panic, lost perspective and then spiralled out of control. The actual outcome would not have changed. The difference would have been my reaction and behaviour. Never underestimate the power to inspire and protect others, especially children with ASD or emotional, social and behavioural difficulties, through staying in control and displaying an air of coolness.

Staying 'in the zone'

Famous sportsmen and sportswomen will sometimes mention that they were 'in the zone' when they achieved their goal. Think about previous Olympic Games and world championships where an athlete commented that they were able to accomplish their goal by staying in the zone. It is the state of mind that determines behaviour. When a famous sportsman or sportswoman needs to rise to an occasion, they will get themselves psyched up and concentrate hard on their mission. Have you ever noticed Tiger Woods on the fourth and final round in a major golf tournament? He is the picture of concentration, fully focused, determined and ready to do his best. He even wears a certain colour shirt that highlights this situation. Famous musicians are the same. Arguably the world's greatest electric guitar player, Eddie Van Halen, spends quite a few hours in a makeshift tune-up room before going on stage. Other musicians, such as vocalists, do the same. They warm up and get prepared.

De-escalating behaviour works under similar principles. There are some children I have supported and continue to support where I have to be very focused and ready to be on my toes. I can't afford to be caught off guard. There are other children with whom I can relax more and let down my imaginary guard and then raise it again when necessary. I feel the vast majority of staff don't like that feeling and sensation of keeping themselves absolutely focused and alert, ready for the different behaviours to materialise. Why? Well, who would like to feel like that at work? It takes us out of our comfort zone and is hard work and often exhausting, but essential. It can be achieved with practice. If the strategies have been planned, a risk assessment has been made and shared then it becomes a mind-over-matter situation. The adults need to focus on the risk assessments and stick to the interventions upon which they have agreed. Back-up plans have been prepared and everyone knows their role and other people's roles. Then it is about catching a breather when it is there for the taking. By creating and placing ourselves in a zone and focusing, it lets the adult continually think about what is needed and then have a more positive and assertive response to any behaviour that the child presents.

Interestingly, I have taken this tactic when training adults on behaviour management courses. If I know in advance I am going to get awkward staff members or individuals that are going to continually sabotage everything I say or advise, I will be psychologically ready. I'm not saying I will be great at managing the situations, but I will be as prepared as possible. If I find myself in the same situation without having had previous awareness or the situation becomes difficult, again I will try to 'get in a zone' and focus sharply on what I have to do. On one particular course I delivered on positive handling and de-escalation there was a staff member that I just could tell within 5 seconds was going to be big trouble. Her mannerisms and how she spoke told me everything I needed to know – that she was the one I needed to have my focus on and the others would fall in line. Sure enough, from the very start of session when she shouted, 'I don't want to talk about this, I want answers!' she engaged in rude and arrogant behaviour. The rest of the staff went quiet when this happened; no one supported her outbursts and they were probably fed up with her reactions.

A colleague of mine keeps goading me by saying, 'You don't really like training adults, do you Steve? You have always been there for the children and that is what you are about.' I smile and count to five before replying, 'I feel passionate about helping staff in crisis situations, to keep staff safe' – to which she replies, 'I don't believe you.' Well, it is true for the record: I like training adults and I like supporting children. Honestly, there is no difference most of the time. Adults sometimes behave like the children do on training, so it is about deploying the same strategies.

Let's go back to the awkward course member who was behaving like a spoilt, bossy child. Half-way through the course she became vocally very challenging and was now undermining the training. My patience had run a bit dry and I pulled her up about her attitude in the politest way I could think of and told her in a raised voice to stop running before she could walk. I went on further to explain in a slow, calm manner that if she wanted to know answers to her problems, she had better allow the time for me to explain and demonstrate. To my relief and slight astonishment she said, 'Yes, I need to shut up and listen a bit more.' I noticed my co-trainer smile and turn away, because during all of the training we have done together he had never heard me raise my voice and tell a course member off. The woman was not as bad after that, although I still had to stay focused and alert. I had met more awkward people and worse behaviour on training courses. The problem for me was that she had got under my skin; some people just do, and we have to adapt or otherwise we get compromised.

Social space

The distance of social space is measured from the fingertips of the outstretched arm going away from the person. It is usually a safer place to stand because it is out of reach of the child's hands and feet. They would have to physically move towards you, which would give additional time to move away to a safer distance or block and go into a hold or restraint if necessary. The space between the child and adult acts as a 'cooling off' area. This area is important because it protects the adult physically and allows both parties to feel secure in their 'bubble'. This is a comfortable space. The problems occur when staff feel the need to gravitate towards the child too quickly and too early in the process of the de-escalation. There is nothing wrong with holding ourselves back and waiting. Occupying social space allows the adult to keep a safe distance and still be close by to communicate either verbally or using visual materials.

As the adult moves further away from the child, this becomes *public space*. This might occur when the adult or child need to leave the situation and seek a quiet place to contemplate.

The concept of how close to stand or sit when trying to de-escalate a behaviour that a child is presenting is used in other areas of adult life. There are many scenarios where an adult would remove themselves into social or public space such as when walking through a very busy shopping street and finding the amount of people difficult, crossing to the other side of the road to avoid a suspicious-looking character or choosing a particular seat on a train or bus to avoid being too close to other passengers. When we focus our attention on what needs to be done to keep safe and encourage the child to feel safe and secure, we can then switch our brains on in the right direction. We can think about what will make the situation worse and steer away from doing any of that.

I was once asked to visit a very busy pupil referral unit (PRU) to discuss de-escalation. I didn't really know how to approach the staff; some I knew, some were more experienced than I and all had one thing in common: they were exhausted and overwrought.

As usual, I decided to blag my way through what I was supposed to say. What do you say to staff that have had enough and have seen it all? I started by asking what interventions they found to be most effective. I got the usual answers such as distraction, take up time and humour (all covered elsewhere in this book). These are all good tactics; however, it told me they were not thinking through the *necessary* interventions.

I went through getting side on when engaging with aggressive children, keeping within the child's social space especially initially and talking in a calmer and slower voice. The staff listened well (better than I expected) and the feedback I got from their manager 2 days later was good. She said, 'Four staff came to see me today and said they are feeling better because they are staying within the children's social space when involved in confrontations.' This is nothing new, not complicated and requires no qualifications. It is, however, an age-old, simple and skilful de-escalation strategy. Getting too close is a major complaint from staff who work in secondary schools with mainstream students and with children who have severe learning disabilities (SLD) and ASD who are based in special schools.

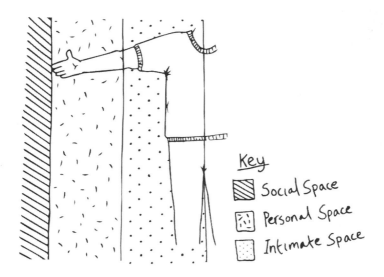

Key

◩ Social Space

▦ Personal Space

▢ Intimate Space

Personal space

I met up with a group of friends that I don't get to see as often as I would like. They are all black belts in several styles of karate. The conversation turned to how to avoid trouble. Two friends said how they always found it hard to ignore and walk away from people who are being abusive and looking for trouble. I interjected at this point in the conversation and told them about the course I deliver where we ask course members to practise staying out of people's personal space, moving to a sideways position and then lowering the voice and speaking slowly. I noticed the heads start to nod in agreement whilst they thought through different scenarios. I went on to clarify that there are five points to better de-escalation:

- Keep out of personal space.

- Turn sideways.

- Talk slower and lower.

- Model the behaviour in which the child needs to engage.

- Show a change of face (i.e. seek help and advice).

Then a friend said, 'Yes, it helps create a bubble to protect you.' I had never thought of it like that. It is like a bubble in which we place ourselves to protect ourselves and model the behaviour we want from the child.

Personal space is defined as the distance between the elbow and fingertips of an outstretched arm. Step into that space and you are at risk of being physically hurt because you are within reach of the person's arms and legs. Just as importantly, personal space is a distance that, when intruded upon, can provoke high emotions, especially if the child is already feeling frustrated, agitated or vulnerable. As an adult, picture another person entering your own personal space. This person is not someone you want there or have asked to be close to you. It may be someone with whom you do not seek to interact by choice. What would your response be? How would you react? Many people on courses to whom I have asked the same questions say, 'I would tell them to get away' (some use stronger language); others say they might react physically by pushing the person away. If the person moves towards or into the child's personal space and is standing square on and getting closer, this will appear to be confrontational and threatening. This might not be the intention of the staff member but will be considered so all the same.

Intimate space

Intimate space is the distance between the elbow and the shoulder. This space is normally reserved for close people who can be trusted. If I met somebody for the first time, I wouldn't deliberately enter their intimate space (or personal space) because it might appear threatening, give uncomfortable feelings and the other person might think I'm weird! So I would stand outside of personal space, in social space; however, adults do place themselves in the child's intimate space. Think of the last time you tied a shoelace, logged a child onto the computer, helped with holding scissors, guided reading, received a symbol or photograph when using the Picture Exchange Communication Scheme or helped a child use a knife and fork. These examples are all fine in the context they were administered. I wouldn't advocate doing most, if any, of these activities if the child was being threatening and aggressive. I would be in danger of being physically hurt and risk provoking the child to react due to the emotions that would be running high.

Sideways stance

Look at the two pictures of the feet. Which picture looks like someone is being confrontational? Which picture looks like the adult is trying to reduce confrontation? Our brains can be notoriously unreliable when we are placed in pressured and unpredictable situations. Staff can reduce their presence greatly by turning sideways. This offers less of a target and therefore affords greater protection. Moving into a sideways position and keeping out of the child's personal space helps to provide a cooling-off space. Standing sideways enables the adult to remove themselves from potentially unsafe situations. The main points to consider when being in the vicinity of the child are as follows:

- Move into a sideways position and point a hip toward the child whilst drawing the head away (hip in – head out).

- Drop the hands towards the hips.

- Stand with feet shoulder width apart.

- Use assertive and positive body language.

This can be remembered as the three Hs: Head, Hands, Hips.

If the adult models what the child needs to do, this can help de-escalate the child's behaviour. If the child is being non-threatening, we can enter personal space and even intimate space. We can stand more directly in front of the child. The adults don't have to walk around with their arms out defining personal space to everyone they come into contact with, but there will be times and situations where staff will have be cautious and careful.

Staff tend to become preoccupied with the physical threat that they potentially face or are facing. This is understandable. Staff do not come to work to be hurt. Over the course of a staff member's career there will always be risks which fluctuate between low, medium and high. I feel it is more valuable to consider the emotions and feelings of the staff member. Usually a physical response comes from a thought or emotion.

Children who are anxious are likely to feel the need to pace. If this is the usual response by children, we as adults need to reduce the pressure on the child and assess how we can diffuse the negative emotions the child is experiencing. This is a difficult thing to do sometimes, because if the adult suggests 'you look upset' or 'you seem angry', this might provoke a defensive response such as 'I'm not angry!' – or the adult asks the child to stand still or sit down, which increases agitation.

Non-verbal communication

Communication is conveyed through confidence.

– Borg (2011)

It is good to put on an act of confidence when de-escalating difficult behaviour so the student believes you are in control and know what you are doing. This is the same for more able children and those with severe learning difficulties – they can spot uncertainty and can use it against you. You can always fall apart in private later!

Non-verbal communication, such as eye contact, facial expressions and body position, are the main communicators. Borg (2011) states that non-verbal communication makes up approximately 60 per cent of how we communicate. This is a sizable chunk, and children will take notice. Children with ASD may experience difficulties understanding body language and facial expressions. I feel that many children can develop some knowledge of certain adults' non-verbal communication over time. Body language is how we display most of our feelings, emotions and thoughts. Take, for example, when a parent says, 'Don't look at me with that tone of voice!' It does not make sense yet we know what it means. Sometimes we don't have to speak any words; a facial expression can relay all that is required and perhaps we are not even aware of it. When approaching and engaging with children we have to be so careful of what our body language presents. A calm, relaxed stance and facial expression can go a long way in making children feel safe and listened to. Our body language needs to be predictable and reassuring. This can be achieved through practice. This might sound silly, but stand in front of a mirror and look at what signals your face and posture are giving out and try to look assertive without being aggressive, try to look assured without appearing nervous and be authoritative without being authoritarian. Practise this often and then it will come more naturally.

EYE CONTACT

TRY TO GET LISTENING FIRST, THEN EYE CONTACT SECOND

Eye contact (also known as mutual gaze) is one of the most powerful non-verbal communicators. It is probably one of the most intimate forms of non-verbal communication. Eye contact can indicate how you are feeling, thinking and what you may decide to do next. Eye contact can be helpful to convey messages and back up other methods of communication. Where it goes very wrong during de-escalation is when the adult insists on it.

What do adults often say when trying to encourage eye contact? They say, 'Look at me when I'm talking to you!' – quickly followed by 'And wipe that smile off your face!' Most of us fall into this trap. It's often more a necessity in the mind of the adult that they need the eye contact, which is not necessary for the child. In fact, children in this situation are not always capable of giving appropriate interaction with their eyes. Children who are feeling embarrassed, humiliated or confused may avert their eyes just as an adult would. If the feelings are aggressive and there is anger or frustration, the eye contact we are insisting on will almost certainly become intense. It will become a stare. Schulz (2012) explains that eye contact is vital because it shows emotion or interest. More eye contact is required when listening than talking, because often listening is more important. Eye contact should be held for 4 to 5 seconds, and then look away.

If more than 5 seconds of eye contact becomes a stare and the adult locks eyes with the child, this makes the already tense situation even more tense. This is how fights start. When I grew up, I always knew which pair of footwear I was wearing because I looked down at the floor a lot. I used to deliver the local free newspaper and walked all over the suburb in which I lived. I don't mind admitting that I didn't deliver to every street due to some of the notorious families that occupied the most ramshackle houses with mean dogs and even meaner people. I would get taunted and jibed as I walked these streets, and if I looked at another male person for more than 5 seconds, it would give them enough time to think and then say, 'What are you looking at?' or 'Do you have a problem?'

To feel the effect of the 5-second rule, have someone stand in front of you – square on for maximum effect – and then gaze into each other's eyes for 5 seconds without making any sounds or speaking but keeping a straight poker face. I reckon 75 per cent of adults will not be able to do this. Once the eye contact has been broken, 90 per cent of adults will feel a sense of relief and then start to talk or laugh. Less eye contact gives the advantage of socially acknowledging the other person without firing up emotions. No eye contact appears rude, shifty and promotes uncertainty.

Think back to the big boxing encounters of the past and remember the weigh in where both boxers square off and drill their eyes into each other, sometimes smirking or smiling and other times with a deadpan expression. Muhammad Ali took it a step further and used this opportunity to embarrass or belittle his opponents whilst at the same time making himself look better, bigger and more confident. Other fighters have adopted this stance and attempted to use it to their advantage. What it always achieves is tension that builds up, high arousal and nervous excitement that spreads like wildfire through the onlookers. This applies to other sports, such as baseball, with the pitcher staring down the batters, and football (all codes) and cricket where the bowler gives the 'eyes' to the unsuspecting batsman who has missed a 'Jaffa' of a delivery.

Extended eye contact sends an instant message: challenge, hatred, love or boredom. In the animal kingdom the dominant male out-stares the other animals. A sound rule to follow is to maintain eye contact for 50 per cent of the time when speaking and 70 per cent of the time when listening. Talking and listening is best when done together. The more important of the two is listening. If only adults did more listening and less talking, whether through non-verbal or verbal communication, the world would be a safer and fairer place.

In general, people are affected by eye contact. The negative feelings it can provoke include intimidation, humiliation, embarrassment, fear, nervousness and alarm. So let's adopt the principle of doing the opposite of what winds a situation up and creates additional problems. I recommend the following:

- Limit eye contact if it is an issue and then increase eye contact when the situation becomes more favourable.

- Think whether the eye contact is for the benefit of the adult or the child.

- Work out if the child you are with finds giving eye contact difficult as part of their diagnosis or condition (e.g. ASD).

- Focus on listening. Search for signs of how the child is trying to give attention (e.g. tone of voice and facial expressions).

- Remember that this shouldn't stop us giving eye contact that is appropriate.

The importance of the manner in which we speak

How we pronounce the words we speak and the volume, speed and tone make up only a small proportion of our communication. Thirty per cent of our communication is made up of not what we say but the way that we say it. Processing words can be difficult for lots of children with ASD. Speaking too fast and/or too loud can cause big problems. The faster we speak, the faster we have to process, decipher what is important and then think of a response. This has very little to do with developed intelligence. I remember one 14-year-old boy with Asperger syndrome telling me it felt like bullets coming at him when people spoke to him. He stated that some words when spoken in a high-pitched, fast tone actually hurt him. Children with SLD will probably need additional time with even less words. Intonation can influence how words are perceived by the emphasis we place on individual words. How we say the words can give different meaning and this can cause confusion and frustration.

We can also determine how a child feels or what they are thinking from their tone of voice, intonation and how they are breathing. When we listen to the radio we can visualise the person we are listening to by their voice alone. We can hear if they are frustrated, thoughtful, uncertain, excited and so forth from their tone, pace and pauses in speech. Sometimes we do not need to see the child's face to judge their thoughts and feelings.

Ninety per cent of how we communicate has very little to do with the words we use. I am in an airport writing this and in front of me is an older male passenger who is acting very nervously and looks like he his dreading the prospect of flying. How can I tell? Slumped shoulders, erratic eye contact and movement in addition to a nervous expression. I have seen this body language before many times on myself and other people.

Depending on the circumstance and context, we use words to communicate only 10 per cent of the time or less. The words we choose to use are very important but still only a very small factor in the overall context of how we communicate. Some who disagree about the importance of non-verbal body language argue that words are just as important. The example often given is that if words are not important, how is that we can find it extremely difficult to understand a person who speaks a different language to us and cannot interpret what is being said through facial expressions or body language? I only speak English. If someone speaks to me in a different language, I might not be able to understand what is being said; however, I would have a good idea of how it was being spoken and the feelings and perception of the person. I might be able to tell whether the person was happy or upset with me by the tone of voice and facial expressions. Let's not underestimate any aspect of communication and not focus only on the one feature which is the most obvious: talking.

Body language is a science. We are dealing with children who have a diagnosis of ASD, so it will not be an exact science. It is just as important to be aware of your own gestures and try to control your own emotions whilst at the same time assessing the body language and emotions of the child. As adults we have to be aware of how we look and sound. Children with ASD may need you to tell them what you want, as they may have difficulty knowing what is expected.

Adults often unwittingly allow a student to control the interaction by matching their raised voice or threatening posture. They can allow the conflict to escalate. Children may become confrontational because they do not know how to ask for help, lack the ability to talk through an issue or can't negotiate calmly.

Building rapport

Rapport is the ability to relate to others in a way that creates a climate of trust and understanding that in turn brings along openness. Help scripts can assist in building rapport. When children are in crisis or perhaps becoming agitated and trying to communicate their thoughts, they need to feel the adult is listening, being considerate and understanding their concerns and problems. To accomplish all these tasks, the adult needs to display sympathetic understanding which allows mutual trust to develop.

I have seen all kinds of different autistic traits and behaviours in children that present difficulties to the adults trying to support them. The ability to have rapport depends on the ability to relate to others in a manner that the child accepts and allows a bridge to be built between them and the adult(s). A climate of trust and general or specific understanding is the foundation for this to happen. It is incredible how nearly all children with ASD can identify with individual adults and rely on them like their life depends on it. I have often heard children say, 'He's alright' or 'Can you help me? I know you will listen'. This is evidence that rapport has been established. I have witnessed children who are non-verbal allow certain adults to remove items from them that they shouldn't have without showing signs of distress. They can enter the child's personal space and calm them through gentle holding or the use of social stories. This would not be the case for other staff members, who are best advised to keep a distance.

Cross-over mirroring

I have used intensive interaction with several children who have had severe communication difficulties, and this has enabled an increase in verbal communication and the ability to feel more secure in someone else's personal space. This is a very useful approach for children with limited communication. Building rapport is different. Using cross-over mirroring (a known Neuro-Linguistic Programming technique) the adult is building trust and reassurance through matching a person's body language with a different type of movement (e.g. tapping your foot in time to their speech rhythm). The advantage of cross-matching is that it is more subtle and the child may not realise you are doing it; otherwise, they might notice and think the adult is 'aping'. Cross-over mirroring can be a listening skill that helps the adult to focus on understanding and feel empathy with the child's feelings and how their ASD relates to the behaviour being presented, such a crucial aspect of being able to offer support.

People who respect each other or like one another tend to mirror the same behaviour. This includes their movements such as posture, facial expressions, gestures and the rate of blinking and breathing which will be similar at that moment in time. Knight (2009) suggests that someone who creates a climate of rapport naturally is someone who matches others around them (p.293). Building rapport this way is done by building people up rather than knocking them down. Children with ASD and associated behavioural difficulties initially struggle to understand the adult's non-verbal communication. Building rapport allows them to become more relaxed and then focus on the mannerisms of the adult that they can learn to trust. This is a skill that needs some attention to detail, and practice makes perfect. I feel it becomes an extension of the adult's personality. Staff need to be genuine when cross-over mirroring.

During an interaction with a 6-year-old boy in distress, I observed that he was not interested in communicating or initiating social interaction. I followed his breathing and tapped my fingers in time and then gradually reduced the speed of the tapping which in turn reduced the rate of his breathing. This had the desired effect of calming him down. He was then able to feel more comfortable to communicate.

Being a role model: practising what we preach

What's that old saying? Do as I say, not as I do! The adult's job is to model the behaviour the child needs to exhibit. This can be achieved through de-escalation strategies. It is not easy when we feel under pressure and stressed. When the children are doing all the wrong things and we are pushed to our limits, it is very difficult to keep modelling what the child needs to see and copy. Sometimes children with ASD need a model of how to politely make requests, interrupt or ask questions. Rather than tell them they are being rude, model an appropriate way of speaking which they can use next time.

Conflict and confrontation

There is a two-way outcome from any issue or situation that will affect the relationship between the adult and child: a negative or positive one. Turn everything into a positive. The more positive experiences we give to a child, the more positive feelings and behaviour will occur which will result in better reactions. Too many negative experiences result in negative emotional responses which drive negative behaviours and produce conflict.

If the experience is negative, most likely it will provoke negative emotions and behaviour(s). It is then feasible that this would lead to or cause adverse reactions from those people nearby. Of course, it is not always this prescriptive and the conflict could spiral and go to different degrees. Any physical responses, such as hitting, spitting, pushing, grabbing, biting and scratching, carry an emotional attachment. Generally, if we are feeling angry, there will be a physical action (e.g. throwing hands up in the air, pointing, shaking a fist, self-harming or walking/running away). These are difficult and unpleasant behaviours that are unwanted and unsafe to the adult. So if we go back to our physical response and do the opposite of what has been described above, we give ourselves the best chance of helping to defuse the situation and de-escalate the behaviour. It is less about the child and more about the behaviour. Remember, it is the adult who needs to stay in control of their own emotions, then the behaviour will mirror that and we stand a better chance of getting a more positive reaction over a shorter period of time, or certainly have a realistic chance of stabilising the situation. When a child has a negative experience, what reaction do they give? It's what is often referred to as 'fight or flight'. There is a middle ground called 'freeze'. It can usually start a conflict or prolong it. To get to conflict, a child generally has to experience a situation or another's intent. This draws out an emotion or feeling which then sparks off a behaviour and this leads to a reaction.

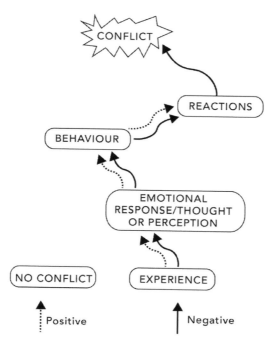

Figure 2.1 Conflict spiral

No staff member is infallible. We all make mistakes. We try to act in good faith and that's the best we can all ask of ourselves and anyone else. We can show restraint by deflating our body language, moving slightly to one side, reducing eye contact and slowing down the rate of our voice. This makes us look more relaxed, calmer and more assertive. It looks more 'matter of fact' and less threatening. There are not too many times when a child will back down in the heat of the moment; it's more likely to happen when their feelings have subsided and they have cooled down. Children in this situation can be like a boiling kettle of water. Once the water has been boiled, it can take quite a while to start to cool down to a temperature where it is safe to touch, approach and use. The same is true for the child who needs space, limited language to process and reduced pressure to encourage a safer exit from the crisis or situation in which they have been involved.

Things that impede the adult's ability to stay calm as well as de-escalate and support the child are as follows:

- the child's facial expression

- verbal abuse

- the fact that this behaviour has happened before (many times)

- an audience feeding off the situation

- the adult being isolated from other staff members

- the adult being tired or not feeling well

- underestimating the child and his or her behaviour

- the adult allowing themselves to be wound up.

Managing emotions

During Team Teach courses on de-escalation and physical intervention training, one of the tabletop activities is to encourage course members to think of all the behaviours that challenge them – the behaviours that push their buttons, wind them up and make them feel close to exploding. Staff usually get straight into this and do not have to be asked twice. After 5 minutes, the flip-chart paper is full of various behaviours that fulfil the criteria.

Here is a list of the most frequently cited behaviours that staff complain pushes their buttons:

- nose picking or mining and 'the green candles' (lines of snot running from each nostril)

- swearing

- playing with Velcro shoes

- back chat
- answering back
- rocking on chairs
- tapping pens or pencils
- tapping adults for their attention
- throwing things
- shouting
- making strange noises
- tutting
- sucking teeth
- rolling eyes or shoulders
- smirking
- not listening
- being arrogant
- masturbating
- poor hygiene
- spitting
- walking out of the room
- fidgeting
- whinging
- going to the toilet frequently
- bullying.

This list is by no means exhaustive. I am pleased not to see breathing on the list. That is what it feels like sometimes. Children with ASD engage in strange and perplexing behaviours; it is how they cope and survive sometimes. Although that does not help us, we still have to deal with it. All of the above behaviours can drive the best staff, with the most patience, mad. If there are behaviours on the above list that bother you, what is the emotion you feel when the child engages in that particular behaviour?

Insults

> I've been called worse things by better men.
>
> — Pierre Trudeau

Managing our responses and reactions is a fundamental component in assisting adults manage their feelings when faced with behaviours that frustrate and irritate and generally cause them to become exasperated. Once the adult understands how they feel and react to behaviours that the children exhibit, they can work out a plan to not become compromised. Three questions to contemplate are:

1. Why does it make the adult feel that way about the behaviour?

2. Why does the child engage in the behaviour in the first place?

3. Why does the behaviour not bother other adults?

Teamwork plays a big part in managing the concerns of staff members. A certain behaviour that affects me might not affect another colleague as much or indeed at all. If staff can display empathy towards how the behaviour makes others feel, they can support each other to manage their emotions. For example, I worked with a child who had SLD and ASD who would constantly ask staff when he was going home. This could be up to 50 times an hour which used to drive my colleagues and I insane during a school day. We would always make sure we were consistent by giving the same answer each time. We took turns to talk with the student and answer his questions and then we would make sure that when that particular staff member was becoming irritated, another staff member would take their place and continue with the same strategies. Eventually we used a board with five tokens on it to visually display how many times he could ask, which worked well to curb his excessive questioning.

'Sticks and stones may break my bones but names will never hurt me.' I used to hear this at my primary school throughout the 1970s. It is only relevant if the person can switch their emotions on and off. Name calling, bullying and banter can and does hurt feelings, sometimes having a lifetime impact. I can recall two staff members in a primary school who were (it has to be said) not that great at their job and continually whinged about how the head teacher was poor at *his* job. I used to react to their whining and get worked up about the lack of communication and inconsistency between staff. Then during one visit I was in the staffroom when both members of staff started their usual complaints. I switched off and only half listened. After about 3 minutes they stopped talking, stared at me and both said at the same time, 'He's not biting this time, is he?' I could not believe I had fallen for their routine over my many visits to the school. I learnt a valuable lesson that day. Talk about self-reflection – I was actually angry with them for what they had being doing, which was manipulation and game playing. I had allowed myself to be manipulated and become part of their game. I had not meant to react that way; it was only because I had become disinterested and chosen not to listen.

Five years on from that situation I became aware of how I am able to switch off emotions and then turn them back on again to help myself manage stressful and unpredictable situations. In August 2013 one of my dearest and closest friends died unexpectedly of a heart problem. He died instantly and there was no warning and no one with him. His funeral coincided with a training course I had scheduled to deliver. The course was re-scheduled to the day before the funeral and a repeat of the course was also scheduled for the following day. At the time I had no faith that I would be able to deliver either course and just thought I would have to wait and see. I did manage to deliver both courses, though. I did this by switching my emotions off on the Wednesday and deliberately thinking of the course content and how I was going to present it. I decided to change one of the activities which helped me to re-focus. The next day, on the morning of the funeral, I tuned into my emotions and let the day unfold how it was destined to be. Then on Friday morning I switched the emotions off and changed my thoughts to what I needed to present to the course members. After the course had finished, I allowed the feelings to come back. I had no idea that this was possible for me to achieve and it got me thinking about how I had managed to do it. My only explanation is that during the course of my career that is exactly what I have done to survive the hardships and often brutal experiences I have encountered. Do not think I could do this intense switching on and off of feelings and emotions in extreme situations that successfully every time (I *am* human); I would, however, know what was required and I could attempt this strategy. It takes focus and determination. Distraction helps, as does having a start and finish in terms of the period of time that is required to maintain this resilience.

Let's transfer this skill to our work environment. There are many times staff will have to switch off their emotions and feelings for various reasons and at different times. It takes practice and experience. This strategy does allow us to stay in control for a defined amount of time and enables us to avoid transferring our emotions onto the children we are trying to support. It's about keeping cool in a crisis.

Internal representation

Right now, if I said to you, 'Don't think about chocolate', what would you think about? I am going to suggest that your brain is now thinking about many chocolate-related items such as your favourite chocolate bar(s), chocolate cake, chocolate biscuits or chocolate-related words (e.g. yummy, gooey, sweet or nice). An image is likely to have appeared in your mind. There may be other words and thoughts such as fattening, resist temptation or I can't/shouldn't eat chocolate. Whichever state of mind that statement has placed you in, it has done one thing if nothing else and got your brain processing and thinking about chocolate. You can't *not* think about it because in order to *not* think about it you have to think about it first. Aside from thinking about a world of chocolate, we have to move on. Now let's explore how using internal representations can enable the adult to change the child's thought processes and feelings into hopefully more positive ones. For example, a child is challenging you and is using threatening gestures – talking to or at you in an aggressive manner. You could say, 'Don't talk to me like that!' and start giving sanctions, consequences or threats. This is a negative attachment to what the child is doing and saying. The adult's words are probably winding up the situation especially if the non-verbal communication is negative too (i.e. leaning the head/face towards the child, standing square on and displaying a tense body posture).

Using positive words or a phrase to influence a child's thinking, which then leads to changing the behaviour and reactions, can assist in building rapport and trust. It distracts from the negative and takes the child's mind off their perceived or real problem. This is usually a good thing. Internal representation can be a thought blocker. Another version of distraction is where the child is coaxed and encouraged to think of something else which makes them feel more comfortable. Children with ASD often have special interests about which they like to talk (not always discuss and debate, mostly tell another person what they find interesting). Ask them about a special interest. The important factor is to switch their thinking and place their thoughts into a positive context.

A 10-year-old boy I know who was diagnosed with autism at 3 years old could be very aggressive and threatening. During the whole of his primary school education staff needed to constantly de-escalate and diffuse. Occasionally staff, including myself, would make the decision to hold him to keep him and other children and staff safe. One of the methods we deployed to minimise the length of time of the restraint was to distract him using internal representation. When we mentioned his interests and talked about certain topics, such as planets, space and Star Wars, he would suddenly become calmer. This was because he had a 'safe topic' of conversation. This was his 'thought stopper', safe territory to engage with others. His thinking and processing were being freed from any pressure because talking about his special interest was a positive and enjoyable experience for him. When he became calmer and more reasonable with his thinking, we could return to how his behaviour had hurt other children and staff and what he needed to do next to stay safe (sequencing and predicting). This non-physical strategy was certainly a better option than continuing to hold for long periods of time. Of course, it would be a different distraction and internal influence for another child and depend on how their ASD affects them. The trick is to establish what works for each individual child and then remember it.

Sanctions and consequences should be given, but when is the best time to administer this? When the situation is tense and unpredictable? Or when the child is starting to wind back down, starting to listen or has walked away and been found by another staff member who wasn't directly involved in the situation and can offer a more impartial response? The behaviour is difficult to consider or ignore because the adult is thinking *this child can't do or say these things*. The problem is that the child can and has already done these things. Staff often have two or three choices: wind the child and situation up or think about what will help by focusing on staying calm, and do the opposite of what will wind the child up.

Empathy with the child

During an annual review of a child's Education Health Care Plans (EHC) statement of special needs, I got shot down by a highly qualified, well-paid professional. I stated that all a person needs to work successfully with a child with ASD is empathy. If a staff member has empathy, they are two-thirds of the way there. The person confronted me and shouted me down whilst giving me and everyone else present the benefit of her experience, which was basically that staff need to study and gain qualifications. There is nothing wrong with having qualifications, but they are useless when the child is trying to strangle you, kick you or verbally abuse you. (Then I don't think it really matters what letters you have after your name!) The professional who was talking about needing lots of qualifications was partly correct. Staff do need general ASD awareness. My experience is that to really start to understand behaviours associated with ASD, staff have to experience this in the context of the home or educational setting.

Self-reflection

I once made a mistake on training when I advised 30 staff from a special school never to dismiss someone else's idea. This advice was met with a stony silence. I shouldn't have said it because I had already worked out they were the sort of staff that wouldn't accept an outsider's opinion, which is why I had ended up saying it.

These are staff that I call the 'yes, but…!' brigade – never willing to see something differently and spend a lot of effort explaining why a strategy wouldn't work instead of spending the same amount of energy considering how to implement it well. These are staff that fall into two categories:

1. Those who think they know everything and clearly do not know much at all (and are dangerous people to have around children because they have lost the ability to listen).

2. Those who don't think they know everything and are happy to stay that way, have given up, block ideas and don't want others to try either.

Staff like these can be called 'a rum lot' – as an experienced colleague of mine would describe them – time wasters and human obstacles who like to see other people fail. So in your setting let's ban the words and catchphrases 'yes, but…' and 'I know that, but…'. This is the motto habitually spoken by poor staff who know no better and by good staff that have gotten themselves into a rut. The thinking has to be 'What can I/we do to make this better?' 'Is there a better way?' So let's substitute the word 'and' for 'but'.

Let's look at the difference between two answers when placed in the context of a behavioural problem. Here is the question: 'Have you tried to talk in a calm manner when she is angry?' The answer might be either (a) 'Yes, I have, but that doesn't work' or (b) 'Yes, I have, and she still stays angry'. Spot the subtle difference? 'But' is used as a dismissive word. 'And' is used as an acknowledgement. It's subtle: but/and are there to either help or hinder. By all means, acknowledge something you feel is true – but/and – try not to be dismissive. For example: 'Did you enjoy your holiday?' 'Yes, but it rained' or 'Yes, and when it rained we went inside to the amusements'.

In my experience of delivering behaviour management training to approximately 2500 people per year, I would estimate the majority of course members think they are open-minded and will expose themselves to new ideas, although I doubt very much whether they actually do. During a 1-day course on de-escalation and positive handling, a course member approached me two-thirds of the way through and said, 'I never thought that asking for help was a professional strength. I had always thought that I needed to know the answers or else I had failed.' I thought that was an honest and difficult thing to admit. This person was a pleasure to have on the course and participated in a very positive way from start to finish.

I had a similar experience about 12 years previously: I was working in a secondary SLD special school and had prevented a 13-year-old boy from fighting with another child by physically intervening with a fight-separation technique. I then guided the child to his classroom where there was a safe area for him to go and relax because he was still very agitated. When I entered his classroom, he became aggressive towards me and repeatedly tried to grab and hit me. What happened next was straight out of a Tom and Jerry cartoon: the child chased me around a table that was in the middle of the room whilst I just about managed to stay a few running steps ahead. This went on for about 5 minutes and I was becoming increasingly anxious that he was going to catch me and administer a 'battering' (some of my children's terminology, not mine). After 5 minutes (which seemed like longer), another member of staff entered the room and straight away told me to leave the room, to which I replied, 'I'm okay, it is not as bad as it looks!'

Who was I kidding? Again she instructed me to leave the room, and again I replied that I was okay and would have it all sorted very soon (what an idiot). On the third time of her asking, I sensed a more authoritative note in her voice which gained my attention completely and eventually persuaded me to leave the room in what has to be described as a 'tail-between-my-legs sulk'. Later that afternoon, my colleague caught up with me and said, 'Do you know why I told you to leave?' Before I could put two words together and offer my strongest protest she commented, 'You had become the problem.' I gazed at her in confusion. She must have been good at reading the 60 per cent non-verbal part of communication because I was trying to put some words together. She continued: 'He was after you – you were the target.' I managed to mumble, 'But... (I know we should not start a sentence with this!) I was okay, I had stopped him fighting and I had taken him to a safe place to help him become calmer, blah, blah.' She replied, 'Yes, you had done well and then you became a target. Once you left the room, he sat down in his safe place and was fine.' I was shattered to hear this and honestly a little embarrassed. I had become what my nan would have described as 'too big for my own boots'. I had been the 'go to' person within the school for advice on behaviour management. I learnt a very valuable lesson that day that has never left me: nobody has all the answers. All of us can learn from every situation, and it is a professional strength to seek advice and support. My pride was hurt and I went away for several weeks to lick my wounds. I'm a much better practitioner from that one brief experience.

Ten years later, I was visiting a school to support a child with Asperger syndrome. The class teacher had refused to let me into her classroom, treatment which I had never before experienced. That particular teacher didn't care much for my suggestions, interventions or observations and then proceeded to inform me that she had been working with children for over 30 years. To which I 'replied', *Yes, and you are still s**t*. (Of course, I didn't say this out loud, just in my head; it was a 'think it, don't say it' moment.) Longevity doesn't necessarily mean someone has become brilliant at their job. Sometimes after working for a long time in a particular job, people become stale, bored and deskilled without realising it.

We can all learn from each other and this can happen in the most challenging of times. When de-escalating difficult behaviours, I often think through and then apply strategies that other people would use with the child in front of me, sometimes seeking advice beforehand and trying to self-reflect to help evaluate the best and safest way of managing and de-escalating the child's behaviour.

Obstacles are what you see when you take your eyes off the goal line.

– Vince Lombardi

Self-reflection is a direct approach that keeps us honest. The more we self-reflect, the more information we receive. Of course, this can't go on forever, although it feels that way sometimes. This is a fundamental aspect of de-escalation. I'm in the middle of trying to settle a child's aggressive behaviour or dealing with two children winding themselves up into a frenzied state of mind. I have a decision to make as to whether I keep using non-physical interventions or whether I decide to hold. Several hours after the incident has finished, or when I'm driving home, self-reflection kicks in and it's time to evaluate. Of course, when the incident is over and I have all the time in the world to reflect on the ins and outs of what happened, it's easier to think it through in a rational manner. In stark contrast, it is very different to do this when I'm faced with a child who is being very demanding and challenging. Still, self-reflection can support us to understand what is happening in front of us and what we could do next time to be more effective.

Help scripts

Help scripts are beneficial because they:

- help to show empathy for the child's emotions

- give the adult a focus

- enable the adult to stay positive

- reduce opportunities for the child to argue or be confrontational

- reduce the amount of information and/or language the child needs to process

- encourage listening.

Here are two examples of help scripts:

1. Hello (child's name).

2. Has something happened?

3. I am here to help.

4. Talk and I will listen.

1. Hello (child's name).

2. How are you?

3. I would like to help.

4. I am here to listen.

There can be many variations depending on the child's level of communication and how familiar they are with the adult. The aim is to be positive and assertive and stick to a script. This is very similar to the idea of staying out of personal space until the child's behaviour is safer and more predictable. Once the child is calmer and more cooperative, the help script can become more open and include more language if necessary.

Help scripts promote consistency and this provides the child with reassurance and a sense of trust. Having only a few short sentences or visual prompts can assist the child in focusing their replies.

Help scripts are difficult to argue against. This is because the language content is positive and easy to follow. Communication is about conveying messages. The message within any help script is to state the adult's intention first to build trust and mutual understanding. Next it is about how the communication moves the flow of the behaviour to a safer place. For example, when a child is struggling not to become angry and is pacing and mumbling, the first step is to show empathy by listening and paraphrasing. Then, once this has been achieved, the adult can establish the other steps that need to be achieved such as suggesting solutions, challenging the behaviour which is being exhibited or predicting and sequencing what will need to happen next.

When the help script is used in conjunction with non-verbal communication strategies (i.e. personal space, sideways position and reducing eye contact), it can place the adult in a much safer and more assertive position. It will create a non-threatening atmosphere.

I recall a particular 9-year-old boy I supported. His father was extremely volatile and often violent. (He once threatened to kill the head teacher of his son's primary school and then repeated this threat to the head teacher of his next school.) This boy's ASD was hard to see. This happens sometimes when there are other conditions that run alongside the ASD. He was very self-directed and did not like to be directed from one task to the next. On one occasion he refused to do the activity he was set. It was a straightforward task that was within his understanding and interest. He refused to follow my instructions and engaged in destruction of the environment and materials. I kept my distance and then challenged him by engaging him in a help script. The conversation went like this:

Child:	I hate you and I'm not doing your stupid work.
Me:	(Child's name), I need you to pick up the pencils and ruler off the floor.
Child:	F**k you, I don't have to do anything you tell me.
Me:	I need you to pick up the pencils from the floor.
Child:	F**k you, I don't have to do nothing – my dad will batter you.
Me:	(Child's name), I need you to pick up the pencils. I can help you.
Child:	Okay, okay I'll do it. Why, though? Why?
Me:	That is great. I will help too. Thank you.
Child:	I am not doing anymore!
Me:	The ruler needs to be put on the table, please.
Child:	I am not doing any more.

Me:	The ruler needs to be put on the table.
Child:	No!
Me:	The ruler needs to be put on the table.
Child:	Okay, I'll f**king do it! (Deliberately takes his time and slaps the ruler on the table.)
Me:	Thank you. Let's look at what is next on the timetable.

This script was simple and clear. The difficult part that I distinctly remember is how his behaviour made me feel. His reaction was unwavering at first. I was thinking, *How do I get past this?* I was not sure, so I decided to keep going and be resilient. It amazed me how his resolve finally gave way and he realised he needed to change his thinking. I did not change his behaviour; I challenged his thinking by sticking to my script. I tried not to give him the option of forcing me to back down and change my communication. There was no alternative for me other than to keep repeating the directive. All the way through his emotions and feelings were at the forefront of his behaviour. In fact, we were both trying to influence each other's behaviour. He had his own script which was negative and provocative; I had mine which was informative and fair. Without the help script, I doubt whether I would have been able to keep up with his thinking and tactic of attempting to force me to back down and give up. The advantage this incident gave me was that I was able to set a different tone for future encounters. My use of a script enabled me to avoid direct confrontation and use communication in a consistent manner.

On one occasion, minding my own business, I walked underneath a staircase at the PRU where I was based. I just happened to look up and see a 14-year-old student sitting on the rails two flights of stairs up. Before I could say anything, I got a mouthful of abuse along the lines of if I told anyone where he was, he would kill me there and then. (This is the polite version; I have cut out the many swear words.) I used a language script to communicate, lowered my voice and informed him that I was only interested in his safety due to the risky position he was in. I received another barrage of abuse similar to the first time. I didn't know the student that well and wasn't sure if he meant it, as there was no way of knowing. So I stuck to my communication script and said, 'My name's Steve. I'm concerned about your safety.' He replied once again that he was going to kill me if I told someone. I wasn't going to be drawn into being dictated to, so I focused on his safety. This was a situation that was never going to go anywhere positive with me. He was clearly angry with other staff; he didn't know me and he was in an unsafe position. Out the corner of my eye I saw several staff walking towards the bottom of the stairs, so I ushered them away so he couldn't hear us and informed them of where he was and his state of mind. After waiting several minutes, two of the staff who knew him well were able to approach him and talk, calm him down and lead him back to class. One of the three staff members commented on how much abuse I had taken. This didn't worry me on a personal level, but I did feel the boy needed a consequence for how he had spoken. Later that afternoon, I spoke to the PRU manager and explained that although I hadn't taken it personally and just happened to be there at the time, I felt the boy needed to be challenged about his conduct because he was aggressive and used threatening behaviour that was not acceptable. The next morning, the student and the manger knocked on my office door where I got this wonderful apology and the boy told me how he regretted talking to me in the manner he had. We shook hands to indicate no hard feelings and I asked him how he could have told me what he needed in a better way. He said, 'Leave me alone. I don't want to talk to anyone right now.' I told him that was a better way of talking and, if he could, to try to remember next time so that he would find himself in less trouble. The thing that struck me was how very calm, thoughtful and charming he was when he came to apologise. He was a different person who was being reasonable and considerate.

I had not damaged my standing with him but had modelled what he had needed to do. I had taken some abuse which I laughed off later with my colleagues and had started to build and gain some trust with the child, which is the most important part.

This is just one way of dealing with difficult and aggressive behaviours. It is important not to box yourself into a corner; instead, it's about 'boxing' cleverly and seeing a way out that helps the child. The child is the most important person and it's often the process that matters, not so much the outcome. The next time, that particular student will know how I work. There might be a little more trust and he will also know that I won't allow myself to get wound up.

Talk low, slow and give processing time

Talk slow, talk low and don't say too much.

— John Wayne

I guess Mr Wayne was good at this. It's the three auditory rules of de-escalating behaviour. When faced with children who are out of control, aggressive and loud – or the complete opposite (i.e. withdrawn and inaudible) – our brains often make poor choices and decisions. Our voices become louder and higher pitched, intonation becomes negative and blaming, and our body language reflects this auditory display. Adults turn square on and puff out various body parts such as the chest, shoulders and chin. Muscles contract in the face and eyes drill into the child. Feet face the child and send signals that 'I'm facing up'. Under these circumstances it is more difficult for the child to process the language. When we *reduce* the number of words spoken, keep a *lower tone* and maintain a *slower pace*, the child will have a better chance of processing what is being said.

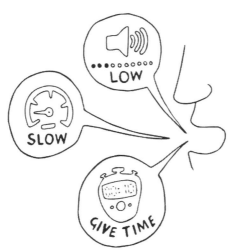

Talk and listen

Courage is what it takes to stand up and speak. Courage is also what it takes to sit down and listen.

— Winston Churchill

There is no prize for guessing which one is more difficult than the other. Talking comes more naturally. Listening takes far more concentration and patience. Children really do more listening than adults. Since 2003 I have trained approximately 8000 staff on various training courses. Quite a few of those staff were poor listeners, and some of them liked to talk incessantly – talk that becomes waffle, mind-blowing nonsense which triggers alarm bells to start ringing, prompting the question, 'Should you actually be working with children?' Talking and listening is underrated and undervalued. It is usually what children struggle with whenever they are on the spectrum. This can be described as situation awareness. Staff need to take into consideration the context and environment in which the child and others are placed. For example, if I have a child throwing an item across a room at me and others, I will have a different view than if I find myself in a situation where a child is sitting under a table making aggressive noises.

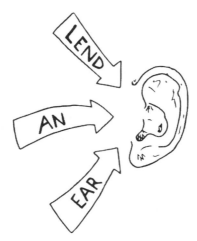

Situation awareness

Situation awareness usually has three levels – perception, comprehension and projection – which are described as follows:

- *Perception.* This basic level involves the processes of monitoring and displaying recognition of what state of mind the child is in or what behaviours are being displayed, and then assessing the level of risk.

- *Comprehension.* This level requires the integration of recognition and evaluation of what needs to be done or avoided. What is the main priority for the child?

- *Projection.* This level involves projecting the actions that have been determined in the first two levels, that is, determining the next sequence and what effect it will have on the child's situation and well-being.

As with any model of practice, situation awareness is not always straightforward or achievable. Nothing in work or life is perfect. Two of the dangerous states that adults drift into are inflexibility and self-importance. By stopping and thinking, then being patient and listening well, we might just learn what the best thing to say next is or, perhaps more importantly, what to *avoid* saying.

THE LIGHTHOUSE STORY

You may have read about or heard a comedian recite the infamous story of the naval ship and the lighthouse keeper. This story probably didn't happen, and like most tales it changes and grows bigger and better with time. Whether it is truth or fiction probably does not matter either. There is a situation-awareness point that all of us can learn from when de-escalating and diffusing difficult behaviour.

The transcript that involves the captain of an aircraft carrier is this:

Aircraft carrier: Please divert your course 15 degrees to the north to avoid a collision.

Canadian authorities: Please divert your course 15 degrees to the north to avoid a collision.

Aircraft carrier: This is the captain of a US Navy ship. Please divert *your* course 15 degrees to the north to avoid a collision.

Canadian authorities: No, I say again, you divert *your* course.

Aircraft carrier: This is the aircraft carrier USS Abraham Lincoln, the second largest ship in the United States Atlantic Fleet. I demand that you change your course 15 degrees north. That's one-five degrees north, or counter measures will be taken to ensure the safety of this ship!

Canadian authorities: This is the lighthouse keeper…*your* call.

Even as a bit of fun this transcript can remind us not to be full of our own self-importance and to think carefully about the other side of the situation or issue. Perhaps if staff try hard to take into account their environment, and influence the mood of the child, better outcomes will prevail.

I recently observed a friend who works in a winery skilfully manage a range of challenging behaviour from adults who were wine tasting. This is a very difficult and skilled job because customers can become very aggressive and confrontational. He was able to defuse and de-escalate using a combination of humour, quick thinking and patience. This reminded me of how adults' behaviour can be the same as that of children when they feel agitated, embarrassed and awkward, and how the strategies to manage the behaviours are similar. He commented on the importance of allowing people to vent their anger without interruption, avoid using trigger phrases or words and look for a solution to the problem. Like an adult working with children, he needed to observe the environment, use humour appropriately and keep his wits about him to spot potential conflict and changes in mood.

> *Praise loudly, blame softly.*
>
> – Catherine the Great

I overheard a colleague in a PRU (when dealing with a very difficult 12-year-old boy) say, 'I know I have already said that many times and you have been brilliant following my requests.' The child was and had been protesting aggressively that the adult had been giving the same directive over and over to prevent him from doing something which would lead him into trouble. The staff member acknowledged how well the child had listened, expressed her own feelings and gave praise. It enabled the adult to stay in the game and remain calm because it was a positive statement. By using a positive approach she was then able to give the next instruction and it was less likely to cause a repeat of the original behaviour.

Think about how many times we actually praise the child when they start following our requests after a prolonged period of refusal or ignoring. It is a helpful, positive idea for the adult to offer praise when a child starts to make the right choice.

It is worth remembering an important aspect of de-escalation: *Diffuse challenging behaviour like you have nothing to lose and the child has everything to gain, then you can help stay in control of your emotions.*

Debriefing

There is a direct link between how much staff debrief and allow positive listening after an incident has occurred and the amount of physical intervention required. The more we debrief, which means talk and listen, the more staff can lower the occurrences of physical intervention. The trick with debriefing is when to do it. This depends on the child. Sometimes it is more effective and supportive to debrief immediately after the incident. Some children and staff need more time. Inviting another person to assist with the debriefing can work well especially if the staff member directly involved is the issue and target of the child's anger.

Debriefing is about repair and recovery. It is the aftercare of de-escalation. This must not be missed or overlooked. There is a lot of important information that can come out of talking and listening after a confrontation or restraint. Children can often indicate their own needs to staff that have never before been considered. Children with autism sometimes forget or do not realise why they are in this position and need reminding. Some children will not care. That is when debriefing comes into its own. Remaining patient and using the strategies that have been mentioned will help reach a better outcome for the child.

Acting like you are doing nothing

Keep your mouth shut and your eyes open.

— Samuel Palmer

Human instinct and brains tend to work overtime when it comes to solving problems regarding behaviour. I've mentioned the incessant desire to gravitate towards children when they are behaving in an unsafe way. As adults it is because we think we need to get closer to stay in control of the situation that surrounds us. I have to stop myself sometimes. Maybe as adults we are anxious and occasionally scared when dealing with unpredictable or aggressive behaviour of children. I feel it is fair and normal to feel that way. At times it may be that the adult needs to zip their mouth, step to the side and view the child from a greater distance and think about what they can do to help. Alternatively, the adult could wait until there is an opening to communicate positively. Hanging back gives us time to listen, which is a fundamental skill. It allows time to predict where the behaviour is going next and assess whether it is becoming worse or getting better.

I remember on one occasion a 13-year-old boy with ASD and SLD kept charging towards me grabbing and hitting. I realised after several minutes this was happening because every time he finished his charge and walked back I followed him. Why was I engaging in this pattern of behaviour? I can only think that I felt the need to protect my personal space and felt I was being insulted rather than assaulted. I'm not sure. I must have allowed my emotions to get the better of me. I was on my own and should have walked to a safe distance and requested a change of face or observed the child from a distance and kept out of his way until he had become calmer. The more matter of fact we can present ourselves and at the same time appear assertive, the better our chances are of not winding up the child's behaviour.

When we take a sideways look and hang back, it often looks like we are doing nothing. I have been accused of this several times, and some of my former work colleagues have become irritated. They have commented, 'You were not doing anything; he (the child) was getting away with being rude.' Unfortunately, these were often the same work colleagues that shouted, got too close and tried to boss the child into stopping their 'bad' behaviour. Sometimes it was because they had run out of patience or emotions had been compromised. One of the worst occasions when I witnessed this was during a visit to a 6-year-old boy with autism in a mainstream school. I knew him well and was visiting him to help modify his aggressive behaviour. Upon arriving in the classroom he was kicking chairs over and was clearly not happy. After kicking over the last chair, he refused to sit down and was very agitated about something but no one knew what. After approaching him and trying to distract him with an activity in which he would be usually interested, he fell to the floor and had a tantrum that would have made a toddler proud. I instructed the other children to go calmly back to their seats. I had seen him do this before, as had the other staff in the room. I crouched about 3 metres away and looked slightly away from where he continued to flail and scream. I thought that if I gave him a few minutes, he would stop the tantrum and then look for an adult to help him become calmer. The other children had been sent to sit at the tables and no equipment was close by, so the risk was reduced. After 2 minutes, a member of staff walked past the door and looked in, stood with her hands on her hips and shook her head. Next she walked quickly towards the boy, who was still continuing his tantrum on the floor, looked in my direction, shook her head, tutted and then scooped the child up by placing her arms under his shoulders and hips. She carried him towards the door and then walked out of the room. The whole time he was screaming louder, and his head, arms and legs were thrashing about, narrowly missing the door frame. I'm not sure what happened to him for the next 15 minutes, as all I could hear were screams becoming gradually more desperate. I was not impressed. I could have guaranteed he would have stood up within a few more minutes, felt embarrassed and then joined in with an activity. The staff member was disrespectful and needed to have spoken with me first to offer help or make a suggestion. Her body language indicated she was not impressed with my letting him 'get away' with this type of behaviour. There was no need to physically intervene. The child wasn't hurting other children, staff or himself, and he wasn't damaging property. The track record of this child was that he would normally snap out of his meltdown and look for adult support. The situation was made much worse and, more importantly, he was placed in a greater degree of danger.

Ignoring what you can

No one can make you feel inferior without your consent.

– Eleanor Roosevelt

When I was 13 years old I remember my father videotaping a TV series for me called 'Great Fights of the Seventies'. One of the fights was Muhammad Ali vs Ken Norton. This was the first fight of three. Ali was legendary for winding up and intimidating opponents. He would poke fun at them, taunt them, get in their space, pull faces and generally try to goad and cause upset. I loved all that showy style that came over so well with his handsome face and cheeky grin. What stopped me in my tracks and spoilt things in this fight was Norton's response. He didn't go for any of Ali's taunts. He ignored all the usual jibes and insults. He didn't say anything back or show any sign of being wound up or upset. I think Ali used to say some hard-hitting things to his challengers. Ken Norton never once responded to Ali trying to put him off his stride. What resulted was a frustrated Muhammad Ali who was used to his opponents being put off. He was used to getting under their skin and throwing his opponent off their game plan. During the fight Ali became quieter and more subdued. The fact that Norton won the fight and, in doing so, inflicted the second defeat of Ali's career was just part of the event. The real event that astounded the boxing world was the fact that Norton gave a really tough fight.

The late great Joe Frazier had spent time with Norton because Norton was one of Frazier's sparring partners and Norton was told, 'Don't go for his jive and don't listen to his talk. Keep your head down. Ignore all his shenanigans.' Norton did just that to great avail. He benefited from staying cool and quiet and didn't become drawn into a confrontation. He stayed away from Ali's intimidating behaviour. His face never changed much if he was losing or winning; indifferent to the end. Ali kept becoming more despondent and then started to give up his attention seeking and learnt behaviour. Why? It wasn't working, so it was no fun and not worth continuing.

Fast-track this approach into a child's setting and it's a good blueprint to use. How much quieter, safer and relaxing it would be if staff didn't rise to the bait and ignored more of the challenges, but really looked at the child's condition and learnt more about the child's traits. Norton knew that if he let Ali get the better of him, wind him up and compromise his feelings, he would let Ali dictate and control him. The more Ali confronted and tried to goad, the more Norton became the opposite. Later in his boxing career, Ali was to struggle in fights for a few reasons, such as age, and because other boxers took the same tack Norton had, copying or modelling his successful strategy.

Starving negative behaviour and feeding positive behaviour

It is interesting to note that when adults offer praise or encouragement to a child who has done something well, something they have been asked to do, followed a request or shown initiative to do the right thing, a small amount of praise is usually given. When the child has done something wrong or inappropriate, the adult gives several minutes of attention. In my own practice I have noticed that when a child has displayed acceptable behaviour, I give a maximum of 10 seconds of praise and then move on to something else. If the same child displays inappropriate behaviour which causes me or others problems, I can often spend much more than 10 seconds of attention explaining what needs to happen or giving further instructions. So if that child wants to get or keep my attention, it would be easier if they behave in a negative manner!

This is how adults can get sucked into giving lots of attention to negative behaviour which then helps the child to stay on the path of avoiding the task or request that was initially given and can lead to tying the adult up in knots. Perhaps as adults we need to measure this out and create a better balance between the amount of language we use in both contexts.

Adults tend to use too many words when tackling negative behaviour. It's a defence mechanism when we are not sure what to say or do; let's keep talking and giving the child lots of language to process. The child may struggle to process or pick out the parts that are important and/or argue back anyway because they feel under siege. Stay positive and reduce the word count.

Children on the floor, children who climb, and children who abscond

The most popular question I get asked on training courses is what to do about children who drop to the floor. I have thought long and hard about this question. I have thought back to what I have tried to do in the past. It is very different to what I do now. Let me put it this way: if I was a child with ASD or emotional, social and behavioural difficulties and I didn't want to follow an instruction, work on a certain task or with a particular staff member, I would immediately lie on the floor and observe the circus that would be created around me. It's the same for children who climb onto rooftops, hide under tables or stand on top of them. Consider the sequence of events and focus on why they feel the need to engage in these behaviours. I now look on this as a great tactic to sabotage the adult's control. There are other reasons why children do this, such as being confused about the request or instruction, being upset, feeling rushed or wanting to hide the fact that they feel they will fail at a work task.

Once staff leave their own sense of frustration and annoyance behind, most of them come up with the safest strategies such as the following:

- Leave the child where they are (if it is safe).

- Encourage other children to move away.

- Remove the audience and starve the attention.

- Use planned ignoring.

- Use distraction.

The problem arises when none of the above strategies are attempted. I sympathise with staff that are pushed for time and have other demands with which to be concerned. As with any behaviour, children will do it more often if it gets the desired effect. This type of behaviour is very powerful to a child. If the child has communication or learning difficulties, it can become even more confrontational.

The language from the adult is important is this situation. Consider the following:

- "Stay there because I feel you are safe."

- "Keep yourself safe and come and talk to me when you are ready."

Visual resources and sign language could be used with children who have learning difficulties. Of course, if the child is at risk of being hurt, it may be necessary to physically intervene to act in the best interests of the child. For example, if a child is moving to climb on a fence to sit on a roof top. The risk may increase if they do this, so physically intervening before this can happen and holding the child whilst in a standing position on the ground may be much safer.

CHILDREN WHO ABSCOND

In legal terms the staff response is judged on what the 'follow' looks like. A fundamental decision has to be made. Does the staff member(s) follow the child closely, follow at a distance or stay where they are and not follow at all? There are issues to avoid in this situation. It is better and safer if staff do not become entwined in cat-and-mouse games. In truth, so much depends on what the child is trying to accomplish. Some children with ASD need space and attempt to withdraw; others become highly aroused and seek attention. In my experience, setting up the environment appropriately can help staff keep children safe. Creating areas where children can go helps to control the variables. It is hard to stop children from feeling the need to abscond. It is easier to control the space they enter and help them feel safe for a period of time. If staff assist children to move to safe spaces, we can manage these difficult behaviours more safely.

Next let's consider why children feel the *need* to abscond. This needs to be risk assessed and then a plan needs to be drawn up to help reduce this risk. Staff reaction can reduce or increase the risk. As staff in this very difficult situation, we need to consider whether following the child is the safest option? Does the staff member move quickly to prevent the child from getting a head start and physically intervene or shut doors? Do the staff need to observe from a greater distance because moving towards the child may encourage them to run further away? Very often, in my experience, it is the environment that assists in keeping the child contained (e.g. having spaces to go internally and having the perimeter of the outside area secured by fences and gates). Many of the language strategies in Chapter 4, such as restricted choices, will help.

For children who actually leave the premises, other options need to be considered. On one occasion in a setting I was working in a child managed to run out of the main entrance when a tradesman was delivering goods. One member of staff followed at a safe distance in a car and two members of staff walked in the direction of the child. The staff communicated by mobile phones. The child's parents were called and so were the police. Eventually, one of the staff members got close enough to talk and listen to the child and coaxed him into the car where he was driven back to school. Measures have since been taken to create a safe place for him to 'abscond'. Other measures included reducing the amount of work he was expected to do and extra supervision at break times. These strategies were successful in preventing further absconding.

Reverse psychology

Reverse psychology is a clever trick in many ways and can assist when children are refusing to move, lying on the floor or climbing. I once said to a child who was lying in a corridor blocking everyone from walking past, 'Stay down there because you are safe.' What did the child say? 'I'm not staying here!' He then stood up and walked away, which was the behaviour that I wanted. A child once climbed up a drain pipe on an old Victorian school and stood on the roof swearing at and goading staff. The staff could have climbed up onto the roof using a ladder but instead said, 'Stay up there for a few minutes until you feel calm.' What did he do? He climbed straight back down to the ground whilst shouting, 'I'm not f**king staying up there for you!' – a good result for the adult because that was the preferred option.

Reverse psychology helps the adult with another dimension to solve difficult behaviours because it uses the element of surprise and distracts from the original behaviour. I once wrote a book on reverse psychology – don't go and buy it.

Audience

The audience! Onlookers and spectators create pressure in our work environment and life in general. I lived on a canal boat in my younger days. I went through a lot of locks and bridges. When there was no one around me I never hit the side or bumped the boat upon entering; however, when there were onlookers standing and watching, I felt like they were thinking, *Let's see how good this boat driver is then.* Whenever I got into trouble steering or the wind took the boat sideways (a nasty thing to happen to a 58-foot-long boat), it was 100 times more embarrassing with an audience than without one. When I did a brilliant manoeuvre in front of an audience, it felt great and I could feel the admiration. Alas, when I did achieve greatness there were very few people, if any, there to witness it.

Have a think about the last time you had to manage a volatile situation or incident and there was an audience watching and observing. How much additional pressure did you feel? When there is an audience, it usually creates pressure. Removing the audience can act as a de-escalation strategy. Look around at who is near to the incident. Whoever is there and is causing a problem or adding pressure needs to be directed to leave. The trick to this is how it is communicated. It should always be assertive and polite. The child needs to see the staff working together, a united front. I worked with a teaching assistant in a special school, and when she needed to get rid of an audience she would say, 'Nothing to see here, keep walking, nothing to see.' It was a fun way of removing the crowd. It was what we sometimes see police do in fictional television programmes. It was inoffensive and gave both of us a 'cover' to act under.

There have been numerous confrontations and fights between children in schools or other settings. I think that in 75 per cent of these circumstances, if the audience was removed, the confrontation would ebb away. It would certainly become less fiery. Audiences prevent children from backing down and can succeed in embarrassing or even humiliating the staff and children involved. The noise level goes up because people are giving encouragement and turning into primal beings who are becoming highly aroused by aggression and violence. Children with ASD and SLD often seem to be attracted to these situations and don't have the communication skills to follow directions to stay away. More able ASD children can be very resilient but can also become embarrassed or humiliated, or feed off the audience in a negative way. This all serves no purpose at all. We know humans like to observe a good fracas. That's why people tend to gather around and gawp or get physically involved. It's worth considering that children with ASD who find themselves in this situation could face a strange brand of socialisation.

Staff can create audiences too. Ask any adult if they prefer an audience when faced with a child displaying challenging behaviour, and the overwhelming reply is no. I honestly do not think staff realise that they are part of an audience which creates pressure on their colleagues who are dealing with the child. It is human nature to want to see what is happening, appraise the situation and then consider what should happen next. I have lost count of the number of times I have driven on the motorway and been caught in traffic jams. I have often thought, *Do these drivers who have this incessant need to 'rubberneck' (even when positioned on the opposite side of the carriageway) ever consider the feelings of the people involved?* It is very important that the passers-by do not turn into spectators and onlookers as this generates a pressure that undermines the whole situation.

The rules for dealing with an audience are as follows:

- Request that any adult who does not need to be there leave.

- Only let adults stay if they have a purpose and can help.

- Let the adults who are involved know what is needed. Follow the dynamic risk assessment or risk reduction plan.

- Follow a help script.

- Give the adults who are not required to help a time scale for returning, or let them know they do not need to return. For example: 'Could you come back in 2 minutes?' or 'We no longer need your help, thanks'.

On many occasions I have witnessed staff creating an audience and contributing to the child's behaviour. Every time a child sees another adult look in their direction or interact with the other adults, it negatively compounds the situation in an unnecessary way. If only staff were more aware of the atmosphere that is created when too many adults become involved. Staff need to ask their colleagues if they need assistance and offer support. A simple script, such as the one below, can assist the adults who are directly and indirectly involved:

1. Hello, there is help available.

2. *Yes, please.*

3. What do you suggest?

4. *Can you talk and listen to (child's name)?*

5. Yes, I can.

Something as basic as this example states clear intention, appears positive and avoids taking over the situation. Teamwork is an easy phrase to throw around a setting but harder to put into practice. Staff need to learn how to accept help, learn how to reject help politely and realise when they need to invite another member of staff to assist. It is a professional strength to recognise that another colleague could become part of the solution. Equally, staff need not be offended if help is rejected but offer again another time. Strategies may need to be agreed at a staff meeting to ensure that people do not feel insulted when asked to leave and that everyone knows the protocol for supporting in difficult situations. Teaching assistants in particular often comment that teachers try to 'take over' and stamp their authority on situations, which makes the staff who may have been using a different, less authoritative strategy feel undermined.

Winding up versus winding down a behaviour

I can easily wind a child up and their behaviour; it takes little time to accomplish this. Winding down the behaviour takes considerable more effort, patience and time. It is the child's behaviour that causes the issues for the *adult*, not the child. My 2-year-old son appears to spend most of his time deliberately causing me and his mother lots of problems by being difficult. I have to stop and think, evaluate the behaviour and decide what will wind the behaviour and situation down (e.g. when he is standing at the top of the stairs precariously, screaming his demands). His grandparents display their dismay and worry through their body language. He continues to feed off this and plays to the crowd, not noticing his unsafe behaviour. His parents advise to ignore his behaviour, walk away and display an exterior of calm and composure. We turn to his twin brother and praise his behaviour. He then decides to change his actions and concentrates on walking down the stairs carefully and then looks to join in the activity with his brother. We have taken the excitement out of the behaviour and shown another way. His behaviour has subsided and become reasonable.

Time is needed for strategies to work. It is as simple as that. There are time periods to which one must adhere. The complexity of ASD can mean that children will need time to adjust. This means that strategies need to run for at least 2 to 4 weeks. The issue here is that staff need to persevere and show faith in implementing the interventions. Adults need to accept that they should adjust to the changes that can materialise, as well as the child.

I am the first to acknowledge that not every strategy in this book will work every time with every child. Nothing in life is perfect. Let us recognise this fact and then become prepared for the fact that children dictate the strategy. This is a bit like in Harry Potter where the wand chooses the wizard. We may not like the intervention and know much about it and yet it is what the child needs. I find that in my outreach support to staff there is a fear factor: How will I manage that? How will I find the time? In my own practice I manage to find the time to try someone else's suggestion, and if it does not work well, I try to adapt it or go back to that person and talk through the suggestion again because I might have missed something fundamental. The brain will nearly always take the least path of resistance, so it is no wonder that staff sometimes baulk at new ideas and think that if the intervention has not been successful in the past, why try it again?

My foremost belief is this: I learnt to ride a bike when I was 6 years old. My two older best friends showed me how. During the first few hours I fell off and hurt myself on several occasions. I still thought it was a good idea and considered the value I would gain from the skill. Then, at 8 years of age, I started doing judo. I was not that good at it. When I was 11 years old I switched to karate, and by 15 years of age I passed my black belt. The lesson this taught me is that I could have given up on any of the above interests because neither worked out for a certain time period. Eventually they did work out due to perseverance, which is the key component, that and slight adjustments. I have to be honest and admit that I have found perseverance very difficult sell to lots of staff – those who have not believed in the value of the intervention and have not wanted to give it a try. I would like them to reflect on the real reasons why. An intervention or idea will only be as successful as the staff member's desire for success and the effort they put into it.

The best outcome that involves de-escalation is for the child and adult to come out in a win/win situation; otherwise, one or the other will triumph. The adult will be the perceived winner and the child will go away feeling defeated, or the opposite will happen and, in this scenario, the adult's position will be undermined and challenged in an unhealthy manner. It is not a competition; there are no winners and losers. Instead, there needs to be an acceptance that the adult has the harder role to play in initiating a positive result.

KEY POINTS

- Survey the situation first and identify potential difficulties. Delay your response if time permits. This is not always possible, although it can be a sound tactic more often than is realised.

- Remember personal space. Most children or adults do not appreciate others being too close. Think about where you are positioning yourself when de-escalating.

- Non-verbal communication usually depicts how we are feeling and what are intentions are. It can display our mood and emotional state of mind. Use this to your advantage to help the child and your response.

- Take the time to pre-empt behaviour; do not wait until behaviours manifest. After de-escalating behaviours, try to offer positive listening and debriefing.

CHAPTER 3

Environment

Adults need to consider that children are partly a product of the environment in which they are educated. We need to create an environment that will provide the best possible chance of keeping children safe and encourage them to achieve the objectives we set. The simple question to contemplate is whether the environment that has been created is reducing challenging behaviour or increasing the likelihood of it continuing. Whenever I visit children in a setting where they are displaying challenging behaviour, the environment seems to be one of the last things about which staff think. Like all the chapters in this book, features run into each other and overlap. The same could be said when considering the environment. Settings should be safe places for children whether it's a children's home, school or nursery. At any age children need space, privacy and a feeling of safety. There is no definitive answer to how rooms should be laid out; this depends on the child or children and what they need. An important detail to remember, though, is that the *staff* make the difference for the children, not the buildings.

The classroom [or learning environment] should be an entrance into the world, not an escape from it.

– John Ciardi

Ensuring a safe space

Interestingly, in my experience staff often tend to over-complicate the space they are working in and miss the obvious. Have a think about where you feel most comfortable. Now think about where you need to be when you are anxious and stressed. Children regularly find themselves in confined spaces or in areas where there are audiences to stare at, and this situation can create uneasy feelings for the adults. The environment can help to de-escalate behaviour and provide space for children to stay calm or wind themselves back down from volatile situations. I have influenced lots of children's behaviour by training them to find safe places. Buildings are not always constructed to help children and adults find enough space to become calmer or 'save face'. Staff are not always open to letting children leave one environment to go to another. Even in the smallest buildings I have managed to locate spaces where children can feel secure and think through their behaviour.

Let's explore some examples to see how straightforward it is to encourage safe, appropriate behaviour by setting out a safe space. Soft furnishings, such as chairs, sofas, benches and strategically placed beanbags, provide wonderful opportunities for children who need to find another space to abscond to or when the 'fight or flight' feelings kick in.

Beanbags are a brilliant asset for protecting children and staff alike. They are portable and can be held by staff to protect themselves from kicks and punches. The bigger and heavier the beanbags the more practical they become for creating a safe space for children to take out their frustrations and aggression. Usually when a child sits or lies on a beanbag, they sink into it and the edges fold against them. This supports the child to feel more secure. The great advantage is that an adult does not need to physically hold the child, consequently reducing the risk of injury. This method of providing a safe and secure furnishing works well for children with sensory differences. The child is almost in charge of the amount of physical touch he or she can tolerate. I have seen mattresses and quilts used in place of beanbags. I am not convinced these are as safe, as quilts can easily suffocate a child and mattresses can be too heavy when children lie underneath them. I think it is about risk assessment when considering how these materials can have a positive effect on the child. Many years ago, I visited a provision for children with emotional, social and behavioural difficulties where they used quilts to wrap children when their behaviour became violent. This is not something I would choose to do because of the fear of suffocation and claustrophobia. Lots of children (including my own) like to hide under blankets and clothes (as do some adults) when they are overwhelmed, upset or embarrassed. Some children, particularly those with more severe needs, gravitate towards soft furnishings all the time. I feel this is when we can train brains to realise when this is necessary in times of stress and upset. This is not dissimilar to how we use furnishings in our own lives. I guess we all have a favourite chair, cushion or bed that we feel safe with and perhaps more comfortable in, or a blanket or throw we like to snuggle under on the sofa with a nice drink after a hard day of de-escalating! (Note: I don't operate a business making beanbags!)

Tents are another resource that can help children, especially younger children, feel safer. Pop-up tents can be manoeuvred into a space where children can hide from the world outside in order to reduce socialisation and stimulation. Tents can be placed strategically to allow easy access. I have worked with several children who spend 20 minutes at a time, several times a day, going into a tent where they can zip it up and shut out the world outside. The alternative for the child can be to run and hide under a table or chair, where it is a higher risk and less safe. Staff then usually put themselves at risk by bending forward to start coaxing or moving the child out, placing their faces in a punch zone or slipping a disc bending over!

After delivering two Team Teach courses over a 3-year period at a primary school where the staff were holding children to keep them safe (children with lots of emotional problems due to difficult family dynamics and deprived social economics), the head teacher decided to place six sofas purposefully in different locations. This furniture was not only for holding children who were presenting a danger to themselves or to staff; the furniture served a multi-functional use. For example, children sat there when they were being praised, receiving awards or having quiet moments of reflection and contemplation. These seats also were used by staff to have a talk or rest. This led to a big reduction in physical interventions.

The problem is that sometimes the adult feels the need to control everything around them or thinks that the child has won by leaving the immediate environment where a problem has occurred.

Consider the following:

- Have you ever embarrassed yourself in front of people you respect and feel you need to impress?

- Have you ever suffered the intense feeling of panic? Feelings where you are losing control?

- Can you sit or stand still when you are anxious or agitated?

We rely on the way an environment is set up to support the way we feel. If children are trained to go to a particular place that is managed by the adult, then it may be safer and more conducive to helping to calm the child. This can reduce the likelihood of having to hold children when their behaviour becomes unsafe.

I recommend that the following be part of your environmental checklist:

- Remove furniture that is broken and damaged.

- Use heavier furniture that is more difficult to pick up and throw.

- Set up different areas or spaces around the setting where children and adults can gain access to quiet, non-threatening spaces.

Behaviour rooms

I have heard so many names for behaviour rooms (e.g. segregation room, behaviour support room, isolation and withdrawal room) and they all look similar. The room is usually decorated in the style of a prison cell with cubicles that represent a battery children farm. I have seen some better examples where there is space to work in different areas of the room – low stimulation but still something to see. These types of rooms are often designed for punishment. The thinking behind these rooms is that the child will not want to frequent them too often. I feel these rooms need to be places where a child can withdraw to or be directed to, to encourage a sense of flexibility and quiet. Besides, for many children with autism spectrum disorder (ASD) the idea of sitting alone in a non-stimulating environment can be inviting, so they strive to get sent there.

Any space in a setting needs to speak to the child of why it is there for them to access – a nurturing place encouraging a safer frame of mind. The space and staff are there to help. Workstations placed strategically can support individual children. These stations can be constructed using a table and chair or cubicles that can restrict stimulation (see Chapter 6).

Sitting

Lots of children with ASD have difficulty sitting still or in one place. This is magnified when children are expected to sit for long periods. Two nursery-age children who attended part time were given chairs to sit on instead of the floor. Within minutes one of the children was sitting for 5 minutes (previously this was 20 seconds). The other child needed lots of adult coaxing and after 3 days sat for 10 minutes on the chair. Just a simple and reasonable adjustment was needed. Sometimes staff say to me that this makes the child look different. I would say that rolling around on the floor kicking other children tends to stand out more. Cushions can be used on which younger children can sit. Some cushions can be shaped to allow the child to receive sensory feedback. Chairs and cushions can be used together. Wobble cushions allow greater sensory feedback and can be effective to support conditions such as dyspraxia. Some children like to have an allocated space marked with a small mat.

Seating plan

Seating plans can work so well in the favour of adults. Seating plans set the tone for all of the children in your class and allow the child with ASD to retain consistency. It may be better for a child to sit towards the front to help reduce distractions. Equally, it may be better for another child to sit at the back or in the middle for similar reasons. The importance of having a designated seat is to assist the child to concentrate and protect them from other children who may try to sabotage their learning or rope them into being involved in difficult behaviour for the staff. I have found many times that sitting a child with ASD on the end of a row really helps to reduce the pressure of socialisation and disruption because there is only one other child next to them and that child can be selected by you.

I had 30 children with ASD on caseload at a mainstream secondary school where I negotiated a policy where all the students (over 1000) were taught to line up before they entered the classroom, acknowledge the staff and wait before they sat down. A seating plan was established for all classes by the teacher. These plans were reviewed regularly. The results were that there was a reduction in the amount of low-level disturbances and bullying, mostly because the staff felt more in control. There was no pushing and shoving to get into the room first to secure a 'good' spot for them and their friends to sit in, as their seat was allocated. This is similar to plane journeys. If there are no delegated seats, this leads to aggressive stand-offs, tactical use of the elbows or 'place saving' in queues leading to a mad rush when the gate opens as people anxiously and excitedly race for a seat. Knowing where you will sit takes away the anxiety and reduces the aggression.

Part of seating plans is how the furniture is situated. Once again there is no definitive answer. I have visited hundreds of classrooms and observed the arrangement of tables and workstations. I worked in a classroom where there were four workstations; two children worked there permanently and two stations were reserved for children who needed access to a low-arousal area. I have been in countless rooms where the tables are placed together, which encourages social interaction. The problem with this is that if children cannot socialise appropriately, they are being put into a situation where they will feel very pressured and stressed. I have seen tables in rows so children are not immediately part of a small group. This is great for reducing the likelihood of social clashes but can become too anti-social over a long period of time.

Sometimes there are tables strategically placed for some children to be slightly separated so they can be better observed or allowed more time to improve their concentration and cooperation. Ideally, in a mainstream class a flexible approach with some 'rows' and some opportunities for group work should be considered. It is important to ensure that children don't have to turn around to see the board, as they won't sustain listening with a twisted back.

Sensory stimuli

A checklist of the environment would be a good way to examine the levels of stimulation that a child with ASD might experience. The information in Chapter 1 feeds into this with regard to the five main senses, the relevance of which is as follows:

1. Sight

   - Natural and artificial lighting. Do the lights hum and flicker? How bright are the lights? How does the sunlight protrude into the building and are blinds or curtains needed to manage the amount of natural light that shines through windows? Can the child see the board at all times of the day?

   - The impact of displays and the colour scheme of the building. Certain colours provoke psychological and emotion responses. Bright colours, such as red and orange, can be more distracting and intimidating. Softer, paler colours can appear soothing and less threatening. (The workstations described in Chapter 6 can help to reduce excess stimulation.) There is increasing research into investigating colours and the impact on children with ASD. Research referred to by designers such as Paron-Wldes (2008) indicates that 85 per cent of children with autism see colours with greater intensity and the colour red appears fluorescent.

2. Hearing

   - Noises and sounds, such as buzzing and humming from electrical goods, can be annoying and painful to the ears. These noises can distract and impede concentration and attention span. They can appear much louder to a child with ASD than a person without this condition.

   - The acoustics within the building need to be examined. Do rooms need carpets and furnishings to soften the sound created by the movement of people and furniture? The insulation of the windows and doors to reduce outside noises needs to be considered. I have had my ears shot to pieces on many occasions by standing near bells and sirens that signal the necessary changes in routines in the setting.

3. Smell

- Scents from personal-grooming products need to be monitored to see if they cause negative reactions. I have supported many children in school settings where they have had an adverse reaction to perfume, aftershave, hair dye and body spray or cigarette smoke residue left on clothes. Rooms within the building, such as toilets, canteens and storage cupboards, should be checked and cleaned regularly. Allowances should be made for some children to eat in a different room to avoid the smells of lots of different foods. Some cleaning chemicals can smell offensive too, and traces can remain on tables after cleaning.

4. Touch

- School uniforms can be an issue. Some children prefer tight clothing, whereas others prefer clothing which is loose. I notice that many children on the spectrum find it hard to regulate their body temperature and overheat. Some children do not see the need to wear layers of clothing, coats or hats and so forth. Wearing a tie may feel too restrictive, and not doing so may incite staff to insist that the child follow the setting policy on uniform.

- Lots of chairs and seats can feel very uncomfortable and painful. Can we consider letting some children stand or sit on the floor instead of battling to keep them on chairs that are uncomfortable? Children do far more sitting than adults. I know I could not sit for long periods of time over a day at school. Think how we feel when sitting on a bus for an hour. How about a long plane journey where we are desperate to go for a walk, stand up and stretch only for the cabin crew to insist we stay in our seat and put on the seat belt?

5. Taste

- Some children may display challenging behaviour during lunch times and breaks due to restricted diets.

They may have difficulty swallowing or chewing food and become embarrassed, or may not know when their mouth is full.

- The environment will need to be scanned for potentially dangerous items that some children may want to lick or eat. I have known children to eat soap, glue and metallic items. Children who indiscriminately place things in their mouth may be compelled to do this or find it comforting. Reasonable adjustments may need to be made to account for restrictive diets.

Again the trick here is to make those reasonable adjustments when needed. These are not excuses but rather more reasons why children cannot cope, and these circumstances need to be considered and, when present, addressed to aid comfort and concentration.

KEY POINTS

- Act positively about creating space. Declutter and remove unwanted material or furniture that is not being used.

- Use furniture that is comfortable and harder to pick up, throw or push over. Consider the use of portable materials, such as beanbags, to create safe areas.

- View the environment through the eyes of a child with ASD to look for potential issues; an environment checklist may help.

CHAPTER 4

Language Strategies

I can remember the frustration of not being able to talk. I knew what I wanted to say, but I could not get the words out, so I would just scream.

– Temple Grandin (1996)

The language that we use is so important when communicating and attempting to influence the child in order to modify their behaviour and thinking. In Chapter 2, I mentioned the importance of non-verbal communication. In this chapter let us explore how language can be phrased and packaged to encourage a change in the child's behaviour. When using any of the language strategies in this chapter, there needs to be a degree of confidence and assertiveness in how the adult communicates. The adult must show conviction and belief. If this is missing, the child will be able to dismiss the directive more easily; it will sound less convincing. This can also happen when the adult is tired. The language strategies discussed here can be used separately, in conjunction with each other and occasionally visualised.

Children on the spectrum can have a wide range of language difficulties which hinder their ability to communicate effectively. The way adults convey their thoughts as well as give directives, choices and information is vital in supporting the child in following a sequence of events and predicting what it is necessary to do next. A main cause of communication difficulties is auditory processing. Auditory processing is taking in sound and interpreting it through the language sections of the brain. In order to have a conversation or listen to an instruction, this has to happen very quickly. Difficulties in this area can be:

- not recognising patterns and sequences

- slow processing

- not discriminating sounds

- focusing attention

- processing information and selecting key information

- retrieving words

- memory

- organising words into coherent sentences.

Some strategies for supporting processing difficulties can be straightforward:

- Allow extra processing or 'thinking' time (up to 10 seconds may be required).

- Support working memory by chunking instructions and adding a visual cue (see task boards in Chapter 5).

- Be aware of processing overload. Give learning breaks, pre-tutor or use restricted choices.

- Teach key words.

- Teach sequencing.

- Play categorising games.

- Give the initial sound to support word finding.

- Play memory games (use the child's special interests).

Memory

I have been astounded over the years how children with autism spectrum disorder (ASD) can recall events that happened many years ago in such inordinate detail, but then the same child cannot remember to transfer one set of rules from one hour to the next.

Memory recall and retention are important factors in processing information. We can use memory in a procedural way to remember how we do something. In my life, if I need to complete a task that I have done before, a clear way of accomplishing this is to think back to how I did it previously (e.g. driving to a relative's house in another town). Of course, there may be several ways of doing this and I may choose a particular route because it is quicker, more scenic or easier to remember.

Memories usually rely on visual and auditory information and can be split into two, three or four main areas depending on the model you are using.

Sensory memory (Sperling 1963) or perceptual representational memory, is the ability to retain information from sensory input (such as a flash of an image). Our minds decide in a split second whether to pay attention or not. When sensory memories are attended to, they become short-term memories.

Short-term memory, including working memory, is needed for mental arithmetic or responding to instructions. Items stored briefly in the short-term memory can be transferred to longer-term memory through a conscious effort to retain them (required for learning). This process is easier with added motivation, which is why special interests can support learning.

Long-term memory includes episodic memories (first defined by Tulving in 1972), for example, remembering personal experiences (this may not develop until 4 years old), procedural memory (how to do things), semantic memory (information/knowledge) and autobiographical memories, amongst others. We can help the child with memorising information by using as many learning styles as possible (e.g. kinaesthetic, auditory and visual). It will help if we use the following:

- mind mapping

- task boards (individual, group or whole class)

- pre- and post-tutoring

- pictures and/or photographs to introduce and recall the information

- repeating strategies.

We use our memories to recall facts and for organisation. If a child on the spectrum has difficulties with processing and organising, he or she may go to the fall-back position, which usually means relying on a special interest or something they can follow by rote (i.e. engaging in rituals). There is an emotional factor in all this. This needs to be considered carefully when using the language strategies below, which are designed to support the child and modify their behavioural responses.

Embedded commands

Using embedded commands is a very subtle tactic to encourage children to follow a command without realising that they are being given an instruction – for example, saying, 'It would be a good idea to finish your work' instead of saying, 'You need to finish your work now'; or 'It is time to start tidying up' instead of 'Tidy up now'. When using embedded commands it is better to sound very matter of fact and use inflection at the end of the sentence.

Word replacement

This is a simple and effective language trick to enable the adult to stay in control or win back control of the dialogue or conversation. When the child says a word that's inappropriate or offensive, the adult replaces the 'problem' word with another word that sounds similar or omits that word altogether. Another way is to reconstruct the sentence using the same words. For example, once, when encouraging a 5-year-old boy (who had a diagnosis of ASD) to tidy the construction activity, I was told, 'I will f**king tidy up when I'm ready.' This was spoken in a very matter-of-fact manner with the correct expression and emphasis on the f-word. I replied, 'We are ready to tidy up!' I could have said, 'You are now ready to tidy up.' I deliberately drew the attention away from the inappropriate word; otherwise, I would have got involved with the secondary behaviour again. If he had kept on using that vocabulary, I would have focused my attention on other ways he could have expressed himself; in other words, thinking about what other words he could have used.

Using the child's name

I always try to remember to say the child's name first before giving an instruction or making a request. It may become a little tedious saying their name each time. The alternative is having to repeat the question or directive, which in my experience is far more draining. Using the child's name helps to focus their attention and interest. It is common knowledge that children on the spectrum and children who are disengaged struggle to offer shared attention, especially if it is a task they find difficult or in which they have no interest.

Consider these two statements:

1. 'Steve, please walk when you are inside the school.'

2. 'Please walk when you are inside the school, Steve.'

By placing the name at the start, the child will have a better chance of understanding the adult is talking to them. By placing the name at the end, the statement could more likely become meaningless if the child does not know the statement is intended for him or her. They would not necessarily be tuned in and there would be the likelihood of the adult having to repeat the statement again at least once before finally engaging the child's attention. This is a simple strategy (the simpler, the better) that anyone can use effectively.

Key information-carrying words

As adults we tend to use too many words when trying to give instructions and information. Any spoken language can be rich in sounds, words and phrases. Take the following sentence: 'I want you to walk down the corridor to the hall to go to assembly quietly and sensibly, and don't make any noise.' Can you shorten this sentence to only give the key words that carry the information needed for the child to understand? 'Walk to the hall for assembly.' This shorter sentence offers the same instruction in a shorter version. What is it I want the child to accomplish? *I want them to walk to assembly.*

When we cut out the unnecessary words, there is less to process. The child is now only processing 'walk', 'hall' and 'assembly'. It is more achievable for the child to put the three key words together and understand the gist of what is being asked. Once they can follow this, we can start to work on *how* the child needs to walk. For children with learning difficulties or limited receptive language, visual aids, such as symbols with 'walk' and 'assembly' depicted on cards or on a Velcro strip, would enable the child to process the instruction more easily.

Positive directives

It really is easier to tell the child to stop doing something they should not be doing (e.g. 'stop talking', 'don't touch that', 'put that down!' or 'leave that there'). I have seen staff – in the words of Ron Weasley from *Harry Potter* – 'driven mental' by repeating negative comments instructing children to *stop* doing things. It is exhausting and frustrating. It is more useful and more informative to let the child know what you want them to do instead. Turn it into a positive statement. A child is running in the classroom. I could say 'don't run', leaving open the option to hop, skip or jump, or I could actually inform the child of what they need to do instead – 'walk in the classroom'. It contains the key information-carrying words and it is more positive. Again I could back this up with sign language or visual cards, even if it becomes 'Stop! Walk'. Some children do not understand what they need to do as an alternative. The adult may need to offer the alternative. This helps to switch the brain's way of thinking; otherwise, it could be interpreted as blocking, that is, promoting a negative rationale.

Presupposition

I always feel presupposition seems like a con trick – which perhaps it is. This strategy is about hoodwinking the child into deciding to do the next thing in the sequence in a positive way. With this intervention the adult is expecting the child to carry out the request or task. 'Well done for sitting down in the chair.' The child had no intention and then suddenly finds themselves sitting down. Why? The child has not been asked. The child has been led to believe that they have either already agreed to do it or they are receiving praise at the start of the interaction so may feel like going ahead with the task. The manner of delivery is very positive language and the child may not say anything whilst they complete the request. Children with communication difficulties don't have to respond, as there is no pressure or reason to do so. These children may need just the key-information words such as '(child's name) sit – chair', or 'good sitting', and then give the appropriate level of praise.

Praise before prompt

Praise before prompt is a very similar strategy to presupposition. It has the same principle. The slight difference is that this strategy is used as a lead in. For example: 'That is excellent listening – now let's pack the toys away'; or 'Thanks for helping – now you need to sit in the chair'. Again, for children with communication difficulties the use of symbols and photos or objects of reference will back up the minimal language required. This is another example of a polite, assertive and non-threatening method of encouraging a child to complete a request or instruction. If and when it is needed to be repeated, the adult's voice can remain calm and steady, which leads to a better chance of succeeding.

Delayed compliance

Delayed compliance is a useful communication strategy for allowing children to process language. Very often the problem with children not following requests and instructions is the use of language and expression from the adults. This is a game of patience. The trick here is to say the same words using the same pace and tone of voice.

Let us consider the following situation: a child who is either refusing to follow what the adult is asking or ignoring the adult when they need to be completing a task. The child keeps disturbing peers by getting off the carpet and walking around messing with other materials in the room. The adult could use delayed compliance by saying, '(child's name) you need to sit down on the carpet and try to listen'. This statement is then repeated three or four times in the same manner, which allows the child to follow the order and understand the content of the request. When the words are said in the same manner, the message becomes assertive and consistent. It reduces the risk of stimulation, which can occur when an adult becomes visibly irritated. What usually happens is that after the first time of speaking, the word order changes, as does the tone and pace. For instance, if a child does not respond after the adult says, '(child's name) you need to sit down on the carpet and try to listen', the adult often speaks in a slightly louder voice and in a more negative tone something like, 'I said you need to sit back down and listen'. This is slightly different in the content of the words and excludes the important word – carpet. Next, when the child does not follow the instruction again, this could be seen as deliberate avoidance, and maybe it is. Then the request changes to: 'Why are you not doing as I have told you to do!?' This third statement is not really a request or instruction. It is more of a demand and explanation. It mentions no key information-carrying words. In fact, it opens the situation up for confrontation. The tone and intonation in the voice is forceful and blaming, questioning. The most important part is the information the adult needs to convey and how the voice carries it. This includes the non-verbal communication that complements the spoken words.

Take-up time

Take-up time is within the same mould as delayed compliance. It provides the opportunity for processing to take place. Take-up time does not necessarily request or make demands on the child. Take-up time is useful to predict and sequence the next step. Here is one example: The adult says, 'Try to answer question number one. I will be back in a moment to help you.' Here is another example: 'Next we are going to start the guided reading. Find your book.' This is specifically for children who may deliberately be awkward when starting a task or have difficulties following instructions.

Holding messages

Can you recall the last time you went on an aeroplane or train journey? Have a think about the order of events that led to, and continued throughout, the sequence. Whenever there are groups of children or people that need to be directed, it normally helps if we break the event into smaller sections. For instance, when a person goes to the train station, it would help if they knew the time the train was due to depart and the final destination whilst considering if there is a need to change trains and how long the journey takes. So the person will have to plan the trip to the railway station, then find and wait on the platform, catch the train and be aware of when to alight. Aeroplane journeys are more in depth. The person has to arrive at a certain time to check in their baggage, go through passport control, make their way through customs and have the take-on bags screened. Next it's the 'not so duty free shops' and finally walking to the departure lounge. Within the departure lounge passengers check the monitor for boarding messages and the final call to embark.

These are a lot of small steps to go through. Transfer this into a mainstream school with 30 children or 10 children with a range of needs in a special school and it can become chaos if the children are being expected to move through transitions without them being broken down into several steps.

Imagine 30 children leaving a classroom to go outside for break and in the middle of this is the child with ASD who does not like to be caught up in the hustle and bustle of the crowd. Imagine 10 children with limited communication and understanding of the world around them trying to find their coat and a snack to eat and looking to move outside.

Holding messages allow smooth transition of communication. In any group of children the adult in the situation could give clear and concise instructions to follow. For example: 'Children on this table will leave first, find your coat and go outside.' Next: 'Children on this table will find their coat and go outside.' This strategy can be used to demonstrate the content of a lesson or assist with children getting ready for a physical education lesson, getting ready for home time and so forth. This strategy is used for giving information to follow several steps that makes up a sequence. If a child attempts to deliberately disrupt the order or tries to sabotage, then other language strategies, such as a delayed compliance, can be used to support.

Restricted choices

Restricted choices can be very useful for counteracting children who are challenging authority or want to do something that is not available. It also helps children to accept that they cannot continue with a chosen activity. It allows the adult to state their intention.

Contemplate this restricted choice a man is offering his partner: 'Do you want me to go out to the pub before or after you have cooked Sunday lunch?' Well, it is a brave person that would ever say that! However, it is a restricted choice. The man is intending to go out and is flexible about going either before or after eating his lunch. It is, of course, a joke but demonstrates how restricted choices work.

Imagine the scenario of a child on the computer where staff are thinking, *Oh, no! – we will never get him off!* They could say, 'Computer is finished; you can choose construction or painting.'

An older child is refusing to finish her work. After giving consideration to the level of work and what the child can understand, staff could say, 'If you do not answer the last question, you will stay inside to finish. If you finish the last question, then you can go outside with everyone else.'

Another way of using this strategy is to say, 'You can choose this…or that…' Visual cards or photographs can be used, if needed, to depict the choices and this can reduce the need for oral repetition, which some children with ASD find irritating.

Restricted choices cut out the risky option of the child indicating what they want to do as a reward and then not having the opportunity or time for their chosen activity. Of course, there will be times when children are given the chance to choose for themselves. Just be careful when this is acceptable and safe to happen. The trick with this strategy is to give the best choice last. This is because the choice finishes on a positive note and we tend to remember the last thing that is listed. Give the negative and more undesirable option first so the child can reject it, and then present the more positive-sounding option which you want the child to accept.

Saying yes but meaning no

'Saying yes but meaning no' is a simple idea that can avoid confrontation. Instead of saying 'no' or 'not now', this strategy moves the confrontation sideways and enables the adult to remain in control of choices. I personally haven't got a problem with telling a child no. If it is needed, then that's fine. The difficulty arises when adults keep saying 'no' and 'don't' and blocking the child's choices. This strategy does rely on the child having at least an average level of communication. Here's how it works: A child asks, 'Can I go on the computer?' and the adult replies, 'Yes, after you have finished your work' or 'Yes, after you have tidied all your books away' or 'Yes, it will be your turn tomorrow'. It is a bargaining chip that remains in adult control. Whatever the child demands, there is a task from the adult to be completed first and a time scale to go with it.

Forced alternatives

'Do you want a banana or an apple?' This would be an example of encouraging a child to choose or make a decision. This is not really a behavioural issue because there is no apparent conflict, which is different to the strategy of restricted choice where the adult is structuring the language to challenge the child. Imagine an older child who needs something to drink and does not feel confident or hasn't got the cognitive skills to make a decision independently. It clearly defines the choice and gives the child the vocabulary to use.

When and then

The language expression 'when and then' is similar to the 'now and next' approach (see Chapter 5). It is very useful in that it states that when something has been completed, then another thing can begin. For example: '*When* you have finished your work, *then* you can...' It's a structured way of indicating to the child what they can do when they have finished the task that has been set.

Active listening

'Yes, we do active listening. It's important to show we listen.' I hear this said quite often. I am sure people mean it. I try to do active listening too (and as a bloke I have to try extra hard). From my observations, what usually happens is that when interacting, staff *wait to speak* instead of *actually listening*. I think active listening is a wonderful skill to implement with children of any age and ability. For those children with more severe difficulties, intensive interaction is an exhaustive version of active listening. To repeat sounds and words or movements over a period of time takes a lot of attention and concentration. Active listening is a process that emphasises the meaning of the verbal and non-verbal communications. My problem is that as I am listening, thoughts pop into my head and then I find I start talking or making sounds to interrupt. I have trained myself to stop and think, *Steve – be quiet.*

A simple example of how we can trip up on listening is when we try to influence the other person, instead of listening. Here is one example: the child says, 'I don't feel very well.' The adult replies, 'Never mind, you will be going home soon.' The child complains, 'I hate this school!' The adult replies, 'I know how you feel.' (No, you don't!)

Listening actively encourages the child to speak and adults to reflect back and encourage them to keep talking. Here are five ways to promote active listening:

1. Use open-ended questions. Try not to judge or blame straight away. Seek meaning behind the words.

2. Shut up and just listen (optional if needed). No one likes a blabber mouth that keeps giving their opinion every 2

seconds and thinks they can change every emotion the child feels. Resist the temptation to tell your side of the story.

3. Paraphrase and/or summarise (i.e. repeat back word for word or recap their thoughts). Draw the speaker out (e.g. 'So you feel...').

4. Reflect. What else needs to be said? Check what you have got right. Help to recognise their feelings, thoughts and perceptions.

5. React. Show empathy. Make your own supportive statements. If as the adult you don't understand, then do not say you do. Best intentions can appear to be patronising and dismissive.

Sometimes when my partner is telling me what has happened between two people she knows I ask, 'Is this something I need to know or can I live without it?' One day I asked how someone can talk so much about certain things when I would rather poke my eyes out than listen to a detailed account of what other people have done. I acknowledge that some people can listen to massively long conversations and then appear to understand it all and engage in an attentive way. My partner replied, 'You have to learn to listen to what is being said and then "dump" the things that are not important or relevant.' This is a good tactic when dealing with children who need more time to explain how they feel and what has happened to them. It may take them a while to 'get to the point', particularly if they have ASD. If the adult does occasionally shut up and listen actively, allowing time to summarise and reflect, then the child will feel listened to. They will be encouraged to trust adults and tell them things that in turn may provide the adults with information to devise strategies to support in future. If time is an issue, be honest and tell the child that you will find another moment or time to listen – that what they have to say is important, so it shouldn't be rushed.

✕✕

KEY POINTS

- Consider the processing speed and ability of the child. Just because they might appear bright or have sound expressive language doesn't mean they can understand and interpret what is being said. Talking in a lower and slower voice can assist processing.

- Limit the amount of words and vocabulary, and consider using key information-carrying words.

- Think about using language in a non-confrontational manner. The language strategies are designed to challenge in a non-threatening way and aid understanding of what is expected of the child, and this reduces pressure.

✕✕

CHAPTER 5

Visual Strategies

I'm a visual thinker, not a language-based thinker. My brain is like Google Images.

— Temple Grandin (1996)

Most children remember information more easily and can process it better when it is represented and learnt verbally *and* visually. I have been told many times by people with autism that they often think in numbers, have photographic memories and store visual images in the brain when learning new information. Visual strategies can help de-escalate behaviour in many different ways.

Now and next

Now-and-next boards are very useful to sequence and predict what is happening 'now' and what will happen after that (i.e. 'next'). Now-and-next boards are easy to make. Laminate a piece of card with a vertical line down the middle with the words or symbol 'now' on the left and 'next' on the right. Use Velcro or blue tack to hold the corresponding picture or symbol cards in place. The main idea is to visualise the verbal messages. This way the child does not have to keep processing or retain the information. The information is displayed visually to inform and remind the child what they are expecting to experience in the here and now and then the near future – now and next. They help to build trust between the adult and child as the adult follows through with the activity or reward.

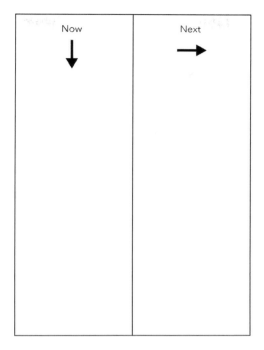

Figure 5.1 A now and next board

Sequencing strips

Sequencing strips is another simple design that sequences and predicts what the child is expected to engage with at the present time and then what activities, tasks or choices they will move onto in the near future. This enables the child to see what is coming and ask for additional information, make enquires or verbalise their opinion. Sequencing strips consist of a set of symbols or photographs placed in horizontal order depicting the order of activities within a session. Times can be added to the strategy if this is helpful to the child; however, you need to be aware that some children are very rigid with this and so it can reduce flexibility of teaching. For example, I currently work with a child who is very literal and who would religiously stick to the times. Question marks can be used to indicate possible changes or if the adult is unsure about what might be happening at that specific point in the sequence. Some people find the use of a non-threatening or fun symbol, such as a smiling cloud, can help the child see the change as more positive. Building in change to a sequence can help teach a child how to manage changes better. It is designed to support the child to process the routine, tasks or activities visually. The first symbol or photo may be of a work-related activity, followed by a finished symbol and finally by the next activity. Depending on the child and situation, these strips may contain a reward, learning breaks or question marks to indicate what to expect. The symbols, photographs or object of reference are placed in left-to-right order (the same order in which we learn to read and write). Some settings sequence vertically from top to bottom; whichever way you choose, make sure you remain consistent with it.

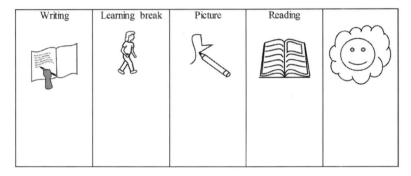

Figure 5.2 A sequencing strip

Visual timetables

Visual timetables are a way of displaying the activities, events and tasks that need to be attempted or completed over a defined time period, like a calendar we use at home to visually remind ourselves when someone's birthday is, remember the time or place we need to be on a certain day and help us remember if there is an appointment we need to attend (e.g. the dentist). Visual timetables support sequencing and predicting of what is happening now and what will be happening in the future.

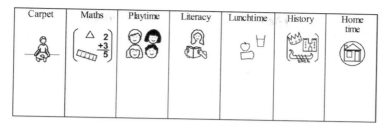

Carpet	Maths	Playtime	Literacy	Lunchtime	History	Home time

Figure 5.3 A visual timetable

Visual timetables can be implemented over various time periods. I have personally designed monthly, weekly, daily and half-daily timetables for use in the home, school and care settings. It again depends on the child's situation and need for routine, structure and prediction of what is happening next and what to expect in the future. The child may need a combination of weekly and daily timetables that interface with each other. Having a general overview of the week can allay fears and anxieties because they can be discussed and pre-tutored. This is no different from a person without autism spectrum disorder (ASD) looking through their diary to see what is happening each day and thinking through what is required. This is a very tangible strategy that can be relied upon and similarly adjusted when necessary. Like most ASD-specific strategies, a weekly visual timetable can be useful for all children and young people. When presenting a weekly visual timetable to the child it gives adults the opportunity to discuss the timings and how the activities will happen.

I was once told how the whole-class visual timetable had not only helped the child with ASD, but everyone else in class had found it useful as well and they were all calmer.

Daily timetables carry significant importance due to the fact that they specify what will take place in the present time. The information can be broken down into finite detail or just give a general overview. Discussion can be held between the child and staff which encourages shared attention and cooperation as well as building independence. Most importantly, the child gets to know what is expected. If the child forgets, the staff members can remind the child to check the timetable or lead the child to the timetable and use the appropriate level of language to explain. If the child does not like what is expected or wants to do something completely different, they have to argue with the visual strategy rather than the person, which takes the sting from the situation. The timetable almost acts as a third person that deflects attention to something more concrete and predictable. It takes the attention away from the adult, which is helpful to children with ASD. By focusing on the timetable, there is less emphasis on eye contact and facial expressions. This can lead to less chance of confrontation.

> *I think setting a goal is getting a visual image of what it is you want. You have got to see what it is you want to achieve before you can pursue it.*
>
> – Chuck Norris

Task boards

Task boards can be implemented with all age ranges and ability. A task board is essentially a tick sheet or grid on paper where the child can see the order of the tasks that have been set, where the learning breaks are and when they have finished. The amount of tasks or activities that are put on the task board is proportionate to how much the child can complete. Some task boards have three tasks, others have more. There is usually a tick box next to the task so the adult or child can indicate they have finished by placing a tick inside it. Keeping track of each task sheet can demonstrate the work the child has completed or attempted and becomes good evidence. I have used a laminated card that is then reused by simply rubbing out the information.

Task	What do I need?
1	
2	
3	
4	
5	
I have finished when…	

Figure 5.4 A task board

Task boards give an indication when tasks will finish. They are excellent at sequencing and predicting the order of the tasks and work activities. Task boards can be reduced in size for more able older children (more discreet) and extra information can be placed on them for children who need more assistance. They can be used for individual children, small groups or whole-class situations. The child can feel a sense of achievement when they have completed or attempted the tasks on the board. It visually reminds them of what they have accomplished.

Rewards

Lots of staff use rewards and there is a fine line between incentive and bribery when using rewards. Rewards need to give the child an incentive to follow directions and requests or to try to finish set tasks. Rewards tend to work best when the child has inputted into the design of the reward. Tapping into special interests works well. I have designed jigsaw puzzles that have between three and six pieces that make up a picture of the child's special interest, such as Star Wars or bottle tops, and every time they are rewarded for a certain behaviour they receive one part of the puzzle that is placed on a card representing the outline of the image which the puzzle will eventually complete.

Other ideas for rewards are as follows:

- Use sticker charts or stickers that label the desired behaviour (e.g. good listening). In my experience, adolescents love stickers just as much as younger children, maybe because staff stopped using them when the children were in their last few years of primary school.

- Use tokens to hand out to children that display a positive behaviour such as good sitting, waiting their turn or perhaps not throwing an item they are holding.

- Give group rewards to encourage several children to display positive behaviours to one another. Display these behaviours on a chart.

Figure 5.5 Examples of rewards

Rewards need to be positive, visual and meaningful. If possible, explain to the child how they can receive the reward and what will happen next (e.g. five tokens means they can go outside for an extra play session or they can have 10 minutes with a favourite toy or book). Reward systems can run dry, so try not to have them running in the background without paying regular attention to them, as this will only devalue the purpose of the reward.

Sliding scales

Sliding scales or salmon lines can be a very flexible intervention, encouraging children to express or understand emotions and concepts. Sliding scales rely on having two sections to differentiate an emotion. An example is a sliding scale that contains the emotions of happy and angry. The happy half of the scale is represented by the colour yellow which is a bright and cheerful. The emotion of angry is indicated by the colour red which is a colour that represents 'danger', 'unsafe' and 'stop'. The number line which runs horizontally from 1 to 10 enables the child to use the numbers instead of words. This can make it easier to express how they are feeling by using the number to represent the intensity of the emotion (e.g. I am a 10 right now, I am very angry!).

Numbers follow a sequence and can appeal to the logical autistic mind. Again the child can focus their attention on the sliding scale instead of the adult, because expressing emotion and talking about feelings can be very difficult and embarrassing. For older children this strategy can be reduced in size (pocket-size). This will make it more discreet to protect privacy and dignity. There is a physical action to this strategy; moving the arrow along the number line which can help the child to express how they feel from one moment to the next. The adults can also indicate where they feel the child is on the number line and a target to work towards. For example, the child is a '9' and the adult explains why this will cause difficulties and the need to try and become a number '5' because this is a safer place to be. The thrust of this strategy is to demonstrate that emotions in extremes are unsustainable and can lead to problems. Life is about being in the middle, where it is safer. If a child is always a '9' or '10', this is going to lead to problems. Other emotions that have been supported successfully using sliding scales are calmness and anxiety.

This is an example of a child with ASD and severe anxieties who was a selective talker. This child used the sliding scale below that depicts a happy and anxious face to indicate how she felt. Staff could begin to understand her emotions without asking too many questions, which would have placed the child under more stress and anxiety.

Figure 5.6 Sliding scale

Another example of a how a sliding scale can direct the child to understand how their behaviour can have a negative impact is volume of voice – from quiet to loud. Again the same principle is visualised. If a child is being too noisy, the arrow can be used to show this and then what needs to happen next. I once used this with a 6-year-old boy with limited language who would scream every time he did not want to do a task. Over a period of 3 weeks he learnt to scream when he was outside the school building in the playground, and when he was inside he needed to try to use a quieter voice. This appealed to his autistic mindset. There is one level of volume for inside and another level for outside, simple and rigid. It helped to reduce the amount of screaming and associated behaviour when staff tried to stop him. He relied on the visual strategy to focus his attention with the adult. Children with ASD tend to be more rigid and 'black and white' in their approach. This intervention can help to encourage children to think about the 'grey area' in life skills by discouraging the extremes of thinking and behaviour.

Picture or symbol key rings

There are various computer programmes that have a bank of pictures or symbols that represent an item (e.g. a cup), request (e.g. good sitting), emotion (e.g. sadness) or activity (e.g. writing). Different colours can be used to highlight the emotions: red for angry, orange for sad, yellow for upset and green for happy. These symbols, pictures or photographs can be shown to the child and reinforce the message and vocabulary. Children who are feeling anxious can rely on the visual aspect of the communication. The pictorial representation can assist in the processing of language. For sequencing two or three cards can be used to help with the spoken word. If a child is not able to communicate due to severe anxiety, they can let less familiar staff know how they feel and perhaps why they are not responding.

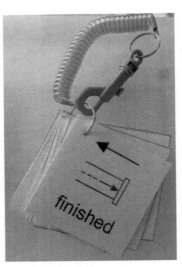

Figure 5.7 Symbol keyring

Good listening	**Good looking**	**Good sitting**

Figure 5.8 Visual prompts

Prompt cards

For more able children prompt cards with messages attached can be an effective way of reminding them what their response to a certain situation ought to be. For example, a child who replies to staff inappropriately, such as swearing or making personal comments, could have a prompt card with the following instruction: Think it, don't say it! The words can be accompanied by a picture that depicts the alternative. The cards are usually credit card size so as to be purposely discreet. This does not draw attention towards the child and helps protect their privacy and street cred. Other cards include messages to walk away from confrontations and the name of the person who can help if they become confused or anxious. The message is visualised and written to a level the child can understand. Sometimes pictures of favourite places or animals can be used to help calm a child quickly.

> ## STAY CALM:
>
> - DON'T REACT
> - TAKE A DEEP BREATH
> - WALK AWAY
> - THINK HAPPY THOUGHTS

Figure 5.9 Prompt card

Organisation/checklist cards

How many times have you been grocery shopping? Hundreds? Thousands? Do you sometimes take a list of items you need? We are not lacking intelligence to the degree that we cannot shop properly or forget how to walk around a store and choose the products we like or need. Writing a list helps us to remember and stay on task (no daddy-shopping in the biscuit aisle for me). These cards run along very similar lines to the prompt cards in design. They represent a brief checklist or message that the child is able to follow to help sequence and predict that on which they need to focus. I have used these cards to help secondary-age children remember the items they need for school that day or what they need to take with them if they are staying overnight at the home of a relative or friend. These cards can be pocket-size so as to be discreet. Ordering the task in a sequence is helpful to reinforce what needs to happen first and last. An example of such ordering would be getting ready for school:

1. school bag

2. lunch bag

3. textbooks

4. pencil case

5. exercise books

6. timetable

7. coat.

This acts as a checklist. This is not about a lack of intelligence. It is about processing and visualising information, in a similar way to how adults make shopping lists. Another example would be how to hold a conversation:

1. Look towards the person.

2. Say 'hello'.

3. Ask how they are.

4. Wait for a reply.

Again this acts as a checklist to enable the child to sequence and remember the order in a social situation.

Visual highlighters

Using the principle of start and finish, visually marking where a child needs to reach in their work can be very supportive in understanding what they need to accomplish. For example, you can place a line or asterisk in the margin to indicate how much writing they have to try to attempt. This can also be used to show where the child needs to read from or, if the child is less able, which pages to look at. Reusable sticky notes come in all shapes and sizes, and arrows can also come in very handy.

Showing how much to write

A simple way of displaying how much writing is expected is to have four diagrams of writing showing a quarter of a page, half a page, three-quarters of a page and a full page. I once worked with a 15-year-old boy who, when given a task to write about what he knew about the Second World War, wrote 10,000 words. He didn't know when to stop. If there had been a visual marker, he would have calculated the task to a more suitable level. Other children may not be able to start until they see a visual picture.

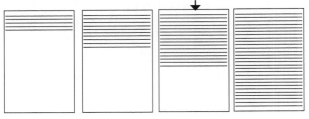

Figure 5.10 Showing how much to write

Countdown to finish

Another way of visualising the start and finish concept is to have several dots in a horizontal line that are later joined together to show the time passing during a task, activity or period of time. This shows visually when it is coming to an end. A photograph or symbol of a reward or the next activity could be placed at the end of the last dot.

Another version is to have a picture or symbol of a character running towards a finish line in increments of 5 minutes (could be a different amount of time). The child and/or adult join up the people running until they reach the finish line to indicate what is next or the reward. For those who like trains, a train track could be used, or a car heading to a finish line.

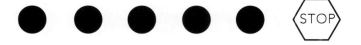

Figure 5.11 Countdown to finish

Help cards

Help cards can be of any size. The child can learn to ask for assistance by giving the card to an adult. It is a clear, non-verbal prompt to indicate they need help. Colours can be used to identify the level of help. This is a simple strategy for the child to initiate help. It takes pressure off verbalising their need to receive help. Some classrooms have these cards on every table, so asking for help is seen as a general technique. I have seen these cards subtly used on triangular pencil cases with a colour on each side and the child turns the case to the appropriate colour.

Figure 5.12 Help cards

'I am working for...'

The 'I am working for...' visual strategy adopts the start-and-finish approach to specify the reward at the end of the task. It visualises the incentive to keep putting the effort in to achieve the goal set. For example, a child who doesn't like writing would have a card with 'I am working for' written next to a photograph or picture of the toy or item they can play with after they have finished their writing. They can see the purpose of the task for them: the reward!

I am working for.....

Figure 5.13 I am working for...

Step-by-step board

A step-by-step board consists of a strip of laminated card that has either four or five boxes into which symbols or pictures can be placed to indicate the sequence of events in more detail. Words can be placed next to the boxes with the visual representation. Start-and-finish symbols can be implemented to help the child understand the beginning and end of the task. Step-by-step boards are not quite as detailed as a task board and tend to be read left to right.

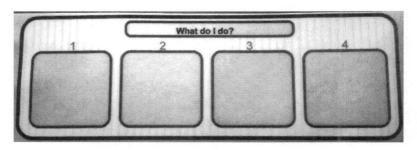

Figure 5.14 Step-by-step board

Traffic lights

Some settings employ the traffic light system of using colours for self-evaluation (e.g. green for 'I understand', amber for 'not sure' and red for 'I do not understand'). This is a good tactic to gauge the comprehension of the child or their perception of their understanding of the task. For supporting behaviour, the traffic light colour sequence can be used to show the child the consequence they are facing or will face. Three circles are drawn onto a piece of card to represent the traffic light order and sequence. This can be used for an individual, small group or whole class. It is based on the 'three strikes and you are out' rule where children have several chances to comply with requests and instructions. The first time the child behaves inappropriately, a green circle is placed on the outline of the corresponding circle which depicts the sequence of the lights. If the child oversteps the mark for a second time, the amber light is placed on the corresponding traffic light. (Visual and verbal warnings and pre-tutoring are used with the child throughout the use of this intervention.) If the child decides to persevere with a chosen behaviour, then the red traffic light is placed on the card and this indicates that there will be a sanction or a reward won't be gained. My experience of using this technique is that the vast majority of children will push the boundary by going up to amber but they will not cross the line to red. I do not like this to be portrayed solely as a negative strategy that relies on giving sanctions. It is more of a visual reminder that the child's behaviour is unsafe or inappropriate. These cards can be removed again as the child's behaviour is modified and a more positive response is given.

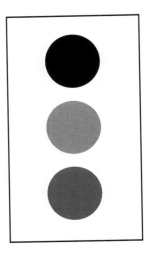

Figure 5.15 Traffic light card

This idea can be placed onto prompt cards. The child is being encouraged to 'stop (red), think (amber) and listen and react (green)'. This traffic light card is designed to slow down the thinking of the child so they do not make quick responses that lead to them being in trouble through overreaction. Different words can be used in another sequence. These cards can be made pocket-size to be used discreetly.

Figure 5.16 Traffic light prompt card

KEY POINTS

- Be creative and design specific strategies for individual children. These then have a good chance of being better valued by the child and can be fun and interesting to make. Some students might even help with the designs.

- Combine strategies if required, but try not to introduce too many at once. When strategies run dry, spruce them up and refresh them.

- Use any of the strategies for the range of children on the spectrum. Visual strategies are primarily about predicting and sequencing, which any child can benefit from, and are the same strategies upon which children with ASD rely.

CHAPTER 6

Behaviour Management

Wouldn't it be great to be able to go to a shop and buy the ingredients that are needed to promote de-escalation and behaviour management? Here are the components that we need:

- 2 cups of patience

- 1 cup of trust

- ½ cup of foresight

- 1 cup of risk assessments

- 1 teaspoon of luck

- 1½ cups of belief and empathy

- 3 cups of teamwork

- 1 cup of humour

- 2 cups of resilience

- 1 tablespoon of praise.

Behaviour management interventions often come down to thinking ahead, being assertive and being confident. Never dismiss an idea – who's to say it won't work for a specific child? In a special school I worked in, a girl with extreme behaviour and communication difficulties would eat, throw or rip up the symbols she was presented with. Staff complained that there was not a way of communicating with her. This was not just about the communication aid; it had more to do with how the visual materials were presented, initiated and replaced. When the symbol card got destroyed, it was replaced with another card, and staff kept persevering until there was a better degree of acceptance. (Some children do not like change or something new to consider.) Staff often say, 'It doesn't work, they just throw the symbols'. This is where you need a pile of the same symbols to replace the thrown ones, showing you are determined to maintain the instruction and not back down because they have shown resistance. Never give up. Keep going until you get the desired outcome for the child.

Workstations and work baskets

Workstations and work baskets can be set out as separate strategies or used together. They go hand in hand. A workstation is a defined space or area that consists of a table placed against a wall and has limited stimulation. Chairs are put on the side of the table opposite the wall space. The child sits facing the wall to limit distractions and therefore aid concentration and attention span. The adult usually sits side on to the child. Cooperation between the child and adult can be increased using this strategy. Activities and tasks can be presented to the child with adult assistance from left to right (the procedure for reading and writing). A basket or tray is placed on either side of the table. The tasks are placed in the basket or tray located on the left side, and when the task is completed or finished, it is placed in the 'finished' basket or tray on the right side. The advantage to this system is that the child can see the amount of work tasks or activities that they have completed and become familiar with the concept of 'start' and 'finish'. This is similar to an 'in' and 'out' tray in an office.

I have worked in a class where there have been several workstations where two children are permanently placed and another workstation is available for other children. I have supported a 7-year-old boy with high-functioning autism who spent every lesson at a workstation due to his lack of social skills. Without his workstation, he would have hit other children and lost concentration very quickly. This continued for the next 2 years with the exception of maths lessons where he would sit on the edge of a table next to one other child because it was his strongest lesson. Then one day he entered the classroom and chose to sit at a table with the other children, and from that day on he did not need his workstation. The workstation had protected him from his lack of social skills and gave him time to adjust.

Withdrawal

Taking a child with autism spectrum disorder (ASD) to another space, or removing them to a safer place whilst keeping the level of staff supervision, can help to take the sting out of the child's behaviour. This can mean withdrawing the child to a workstation area, a low-arousal area of the room or just outside of the place where the child is experiencing difficulty. Sometimes this works best when the withdrawal area is personalised for the child and is a place recognised by or chosen by the child. Children with limited communication often take themselves off to a certain place anyway, which clearly indicates their preferred option. Withdrawal does require adult supervision and direction. Once the inappropriate behaviour or anxiety has passed and the emotions have become positive, the child and adult have the option of returning to the previous place or situation. It is a temporary measure that relieves pressure on both adult and child. For children with sensory sensitivities, withdrawal can help to reduce overstimulation, noise levels and removes them from the busyness of the environment.

Time out

Time out needs to be recorded as part of a risk assessment and/or behaviour plan. This is because the adult may not be supervising the child for a period of time. For example, the child becomes very stressed and upset and needs to go to a place that affords more privacy or has less sensory stimuli. When placed in time out, the child is being removed from an activity or situation with which they cannot cope. The time-out area needs to be very carefully considered, so as to be in the best interests of the child. This strategy is not a punishment; it is implemented to support the child through a stressful and pressurised situation. The space or place the child goes to needs to feel safe and give reassurance. Sometimes this place needs to be adapted and may be used for a range of purposes (e.g.

book corner, sensory room or a beanbag under a stairwell). This is a strategy that needs to be reviewed regularly and used in conjunction with other strategies such as restricted choices.

Humour

If staff did not use humour as a de-escalation tactic, they would probably be taken away by people in white coats. Humour is a method that needs to be well thought out; otherwise, it may become patronising, humiliating and can easily turn into sarcasm. Children need to reach a certain stage of development to understand humour, and this can often be more problematic to even the most intelligent autistic child. That should not put us off using humour. Just be careful and think it through in advance, if possible, because children on the spectrum can be anxious and have different perceptions. They often struggle with sarcasm due to their literal interpretation. I have found that most children with ASD appreciate adults who can laugh at themselves.

Negotiation

Negotiation is an important skill. Whilst negotiating the adult needs to be prepared, maintain integrity and remain in control of their own emotions. The adult is negotiating on two fronts: themselves and the child. I mention this strategic point because usually when we try to negotiate, it is because we are trying to secure a win over someone else, convince another person or protect something of value. When negotiating with children with ASD, remaining patient is a vital skill. Rigid and literal thinking will get in the way. Children diagnosed with ASD often feel the need to protect themselves. Some children have learnt behaviour, and negotiation can assist in challenging thinking and feelings.

The trick to negotiation is to place yourself in the child's position and see it from their point of view (empathy). Persuading and influencing are key elements. All the other aspects, use of voice and drawing out their response, building trust and delivering the message in a calm manner will help to achieve this. Very often the child tends to argue against what the adult needs to happen.

They stay on their own agenda. This is when the other option or options play their part, such as using language strategies like forced alternatives or restricted choices.

An example of negotiation

A 14-year-old girl who has ASD and a visual impairment does not agree that I or any of the adults in her school can help her to stop verbally abusing the staff. We had a period where I suggested several strategies that I felt would help. She disagreed and did not see how this could possibly happen. This is where I went into negotiation and recalled how I had helped in the past. My voice never changed in pitch, volume and speed. I went through the strategies, such as a quiet withdrawal area and a large visual card to encourage her to 'stop, think and react', and talked through how they would assist both of us. When negotiating, the trick is to afford both parties a solution. When she disagreed, I stayed on the same path and re-sold my ideas and reinforced why they could help. This went back and forth for what seemed to be a long time (actually only 10 minutes) until she agreed to give it a try. There has to be a measurable outcome and a clause to stop the strategy if either of the parties is not convinced. Praise is fundamental in convincing the child they can benefit from your ideas.

Planned ignoring

I mentioned earlier that when I am de-escalating a child's behaviour, it can appear to others that I am doing nothing; however, de-escalation is not about putting on a show – it is usually more subtle. Planned ignoring is a good example of this style of de-escalation. It is a simple strategy of paying little or no attention to the child and their behaviour (if safety permits). The advantage of this is that the child can see or sense that the adult is not willing to be sabotaged and drawn into a battle of wills. The adult can avoid the confrontation that the child is seeking. The other main advantage is that because the adult is purposely disregarding the child's behaviour, the child finds it more difficult to become stimulated and excited. These two emotions help the behaviour to continue. Planned ignoring helps the adults hide their displeasure and disapproval, and more importantly, it discourages them from saying things that they might later regret or the child will use to fire back. The best way of deploying this strategy is to act out a perfect poker face and really resist the temptation of gazing in the child's direction. This means taking all your non-verbal communication off the child and starving them of *any* attention. Planned ignoring is not stealing the odd look or waiting for the child to look away and then gaze at them. The adult must continue doing what was planned and not engage with the particular child. There is no time limit to this intervention. This is a useful strategy when children are running off from staff and when they are lying on the floor. Rather than engage and confront, withdraw and reduce involvement. Another advantage is that it allows the adult to think about the next step that would help manage the situation.

Contingent touch

Contingent touch is a supportive, light touch which can offer reassurance or comfort and is not restrictive, such as an arm around the shoulder, or to connect to another person, such as a gentle tap on the arm. There have been several studies on contingent touch over the past 30 years including one by Wheldall *et al.* (1986) and most have resulted in similar conclusions. The effects on children's behaviour in all cases were to decrease disruptive behaviour and to increase on-task behaviour. Field (1999) studied adolescent children in Miami and Paris. The children in Paris spent more time kissing, hugging and leaning against their peers than did their American counterparts, who displayed more self-touching and aggressive verbal and physical behaviour. These results were repeated when observing preschoolers. The American children were more aggressive towards their peers and parents, and they showed less touching. Physical touch goes hand in hand (no pun intended) with verbal interaction. The two aspects work together very well. It would be wonderful to see staff, irrespective of their nationality, use more contingent touch to reassure and back up their verbalisation. Research by Guerrero *et al.* (2011) suggests that we feel more connected to someone if they touch us. This can be achieved by using the hand to touch the shoulder, elbow, holding hands, shaking hands and high fives. Of course, we have to be mindful of children who do not appreciate touch of any kind.

Transfer adult (change of face)

I did a Team Teach training session in a special school once where a very experienced staff member approached me half-way through the day and said she had been there for 20 years and had never seen the value in removing herself from a volatile situation and receiving help from others. She went on to say, 'I do now see this as a professional strength.' I thought that it was brilliant to admit it and change her mindset and therefore her practice, despite her being a very experienced teacher. She was still willing to learn, which is a real professional strength. As I explained in Chapter 2, it is easier and seems more appropriate to keep getting further involved than withdraw from the situation to enable another staff member to take control of it. The original person involved does not always become a target, but a fresh face can help defuse situations and the newcomer can prepare themselves for the emotional impact whilst allowing the other to take a break from it all. They may just reinforce what the first person said or add more dialogue. They may know the child's interests and calm them. It is important to ensure that there not be too many adults involved, as they can become an audience.

Success reminder

The success reminder is a very positive strategy and one of which children can be very appreciative. Lots of children with ASD can forget what they have done well and how far they have improved when they are in a constant battle to achieve and get things right according to the land of the 'norms'. Due to the fact that many children on the spectrum find it hard to generalise, reminding them of previous successes, whether recently or in the more distant past, can help to manage their behaviour more positively. For example, 'You listened really well to the teacher's instructions in the maths lesson yesterday. You did this by...'; or for a child with extreme difficulties using signing or objects of reference to demonstrate what they did well. What the adult is doing with this strategy is verbally telling or visually showing what the child has done well so far.

Consequences

Oh dear, oh dear! Suffering the consequences of problematic behaviour is difficult for children with ASD and their parents. The only thing that gets me outraged is when the child or parent hides behind the condition and diagnosis. Yes, it is a reason but not an excuse. Consequences are important. The trick is for the adults not to overplay them. Consequences can be set out before the child does something inappropriate. Letting the child know what will happen if they persevere with problematic behaviour may have the desired effect because children with ASD can lack the skills to sequence and predict. This is a fair way of helping the child because they have the chance to avoid a consequence. The next trick is to choose a consequence or sanction that will instil the desired response. I supported a child who was told by the head teacher that if he hurt a member of staff, he would be sent home. So what did he do? At 9 a.m. every morning he would kick a member of staff and be sent home, a place where he preferred to be. We have to be careful not to go into punishment. A better sanction or consequence would have been for him to work elsewhere in the school and limit some of the activities he really liked to do (e.g. computer).

Teach/model behaviour

Rather than question the child's actions and feelings, acknowledge their starting point. Lots of children with ASD do not comprehend what they need to do to help themselves or to engage in a safe and appropriate manner. Let us model what they need to accomplish and teach the basic skills that are needed. This takes patience and perseverance. For example, a child who refuses to follow a request, whether verbal or visual, can learn from the adults around them by their modelling of the language and how they use their social interaction skills to encourage and direct the child. What can happen is that staff can start to question and demand because this is quicker, but it may lead to an unnecessary confrontation. The trick here is for the adult to *model what they expect*. If a child talks to you inappropriately, model the appropriate words and tone and give the child a chance to adjust.

'I' messages

Saying 'I' instead of 'you' can help avoid confrontation. Contemplate these two examples:

1. 'You need to sit down in your chair safely' (when the child is wandering around the room instead of sitting).

2. '(child's name), I feel it is safer to sit in the chair.'

Both sentences are making the same request. The second sentence is less personal and non-confrontational. Statements like 'You are doing this' or 'You have done that' conjure up negativity. Using 'I' messages allows the adult to take ownership of the message they are conveying. Here is another example of the difference: 'You are being rude' or '(child's name), I feel that is rude'.

This is a known technique when supporting children to develop their self-esteem. If you say, 'That's a great picture', a child can say, 'No it isn't, I'm rubbish', and they may even destroy it. If you say, 'I really like that picture', they have less opportunity to disagree, as it is your opinion. If they do disagree, you can reinforce it by saying, 'Well, *I* like it'.

Take your pick: none of us like to be pulled up and found out, and the more friendly and direct we can be, the better it is for the child. Also, using the word 'you' all the time takes away the sociable aspect of communicating. Who wants to be called 'you'? Remember to take into consideration the fact that children with ASD usually need their attention focused when being requested to listen to a directive.

Reduce pressure

Most children with autism that I have supported are usually more stressed than the average person. Anxieties abound and confusion easily kicks in. Reducing pressure in a variety of ways helps with processing, sequencing and general happiness. Examples of this are as follows:

- *Reduce the amount of work the child may have to complete.* For example, support a teenage boy with autism who is brilliant at maths by directing him to complete all of the even-numbered questions so he does half the work and finishes at the bottom of the page like everyone else. (He didn't see the point in answering all the questions.)

- *'I do, we do, you do'.* If a child is refusing to cooperate or is anxious about starting or failing a task, the adults complete the first part, the child and adult complete the next part together and then the child is encouraged to try on their own. More often than not, the child gains confidence watching the adult, realises they can do it themselves and goes straight to doing it themselves. The 'I'm not doing it!' can be counteracted by saying, 'I'm not asking you to – I want you to watch *me* do it'.

- *Use start and finish.* Mark how much they are expected to complete by using start and finish either verbally or visually.

- *Reduce the activity or timetable.* Limit the activities or tasks by time. Negotiate reduced timetables at school (e.g. morning only) and then have a plan to increase to more time when the child is more able to cope. This can seem to be a backwards step, but it has been proven to work time and again to maintain a placement in mainstream schools rather than be permanently excluded and need alternative provision.

- *Allow more time to complete an activity or work task.* Extra time can relax the child and allow them to catch up. (Just think about the deadlines we face and the pressure that mounts when we are running out of time.)

Learning breaks

Learning breaks are such an easy strategy to implement and are usually well received by the child. The purpose of this strategy is to give the child the chance to take a breather from the setting routine or the work that they are expected to complete. The length of the breaks can vary. Some children need a longer time than others, so much depends on the set of circumstances. Sometimes it is an actual physical break away from an environment or to get away from other people, but mostly it is to be able to take time away from work tasks.

Two examples of learning breaks are as follows:

1. A child following a task board or timetable (see Chapter 5), after completing two tasks, is allowed a 5-minute break where they can have the option of sitting quietly, talking to an adult or reading a comic or book. After the break, the expectation for the child will be to continue to attempt the next activity or task from the task board or timetable. This break allows the child to refresh their concentration.

2. A child who has difficulty with transitions is given a learning break towards the end of a lesson or activity before the next lesson or activity starts. Again this allows the child to refresh their concentration and attention span. It prepares them for the next part of their routine and may enable them to accomplish the transition without having to compete with the other children.

As adults we automatically build in learning breaks. We have a sit down and a cup of tea between doing jobs.

The importance of being careful about making presumptions

Presumption is a very easy path to walk down, and then suddenly you realise that what you presumed was actually something completely different. Due to ASD being complex and confusing, it is worth considering all aspects of why a child may behave in a particular manner. It is definitely a good idea to find out from parents, carers and other family members what is going on at home. The smallest change can provoke a big reaction and change in behaviour. I worked with one 11-year-old boy who, if he was not the first person in his home to get up in the morning, it would cause a dramatic change in his behaviour. Staff at his school wasted a lot of time thinking about the triggers behind the change in behaviour at school, the cause of which became clear following a discussion with his family.

People often forget to consider the uneven profile of students with ASD and presume that they can do things and understand more than they can sometimes. A child might be an excellent reader, but that does not necessarily mean that they know what to do in social situations; they can recite the rules but may not understand them.

The person upon whom the character Raymond in the film *Rain Man* was based had a brilliant mind for dates but needed help with personal care and how to structure a conversation. It is dangerous to presume that a person should or can do something without finding out for sure. Children with behavioural difficulties are brilliant at hiding their weaknesses and avoiding tasks they cannot do.

Change

Who likes change? Those of us who have worked in education for more than 3 years will have experienced more changes than you can shake a stick at. During my time in an outreach team over an 8½-year period, the name of the team and the department the team was associated with changed about seven times. Acronyms abound, and one of the last names they used spelled EDJIT so it needed changing again and again. Organisations such as local or state governments love making changes all the time because it actually hides the real things that people need to be doing. People have a lot of change in their personal lives such as moving house, buying a car, going on holiday, bereavement and changing jobs. It is nothing new to accept and adapt to change. In our work lives other people tend to make the changes and we are often left out of the decisions that create change. Petronius Arbiter (born 27 AD), a Roman governor of Britain, as often misquoted as saying: 'We trained hard but every time we were beginning to form up in teams we would be re-organised.' He went on to say: 'I was to learn later that any new situation is met by re-organising. What a wonderful method it can be for creating an illusion of progress, whilst producing confusion, inefficiency and demoralisation.' (Petronius Arbiter committed suicide in 65 AD.) Charlton Ogburn also commented on constant reorganisation creating an illusion of progress, but actually creating confusion and inefficiency, as well as demoralising people in the process (Ogburn 1957).

Checklists, visual timetables, social stories and task boards are all very useful ways of explaining changes. Information can be given verbally as well, but having a visual backup helps to reinforce the information and makes it harder for the child to argue that they were not aware of the change. Plan changes in advance, if you can;

otherwise, if it is at short notice, visualise what is changing and sometimes expect the kick back from the child. After all, it is normal to be disappointed or upset when there is an expectation of engaging in an activity or task and then it does not happen. I feel it is a fallacy that all children with ASD cannot accept change. Some children find it difficult but most can accept change when it is predicted, sequenced and supported sensitively.

KEY POINTS

- Accept the behaviour for what it is. It is rarely initiated to annoy you. It will become harder to manage when the child becomes aware it is compromising your emotions.

- Accept and consider all ideas and be flexible in your approach.

- Allow enough time for the strategies to embed and work in everyone's favour. Generally, any behaviour strategy needs to be in place for at least 2 weeks to be given the opportunity to succeed.

CHAPTER 7

Risk Assessment, Guidance and Legalities

In 2011, I completed a study that explored the benefits of Team Teach training for staff working within an autism outreach team. They were asked to comment on how safe they felt when dealing with incidents of challenging behaviour before and after the training. Team Teach is a holistic approach which trains staff in three main areas: de-escalation and communication strategies, restrictive physical interventions and the legal framework. Course members are also given guidance on how to complete 'planned and dynamic risk assessments' which Allen (2003) recommends for staff who are exposed to challenging situations with children. The conclusions drawn from this research show the importance of staff feeling safe when dealing with challenging behaviour. Their emotions are an important factor in how they choose to manage difficult situations. There was reluctance on the part of these staff to engage in physical interventions for good reasons, but when it is needed, as a last resort, they felt it was important to know how to hold safely and within the legal framework (if required). The outreach team were unanimous about the benefit of the training for them and also reported their belief that the children on their caseload at risk of exclusion from their setting had decreased as a result. They were all reassured to know their best and most robust legal defence.

I feel staff working with children with autism spectrum disorder (ASD) have a greater chance of finding themselves in a position where they may have to decide whether they need to physically intervene. If and when this happens, it is incredibly important that staff know the legal implications and the significance of making risk assessments. Legalities, risk assessments and guidance mix and match together; occasionally they separate but they mostly overlap and integrate. I will discuss each area individually and then let them naturally overlap.

Risk assessments

All staff have a duty of care to keep children safe. Adults can take reasonable action to keep children safe – from themselves and from others. It is not always possible to predict all risks related to a specific behaviour of a child. When an unforeseeable risk presents itself, a *dynamic risk assessment* can be used to support staff in conducting a quick risk assessment and then act in the best interests of both the child and those of others in the school. Once a risk has been identified, or if the risk is already known, a *planned risk assessment* needs to be put in writing. If physical touch or restraint is required, a *risk reduction plan* (see Appendix) needs to be recorded by staff who work closely with the child using their knowledge of the child's behaviour and the environment in which they are working.

It would be unrealistic to expect staff to guarantee 100 per cent that they can protect every child with whom they work. Unpredictable behaviour and human error will see to that. All the adults can do is act in good faith and do their very best. No one can ask for more than that.

Dynamic risk assessments

My nan once made a great dynamic risk assessment. About 7 years before her death, she decided that she did not want to burden my mother and aunty with the cost of her funeral. As she was much loved and respected, members of her family did not wish to contemplate her passing away. So my nan booked an appointment with a local funeral director and asked her two daughters to accompany her to arrange and pay for the funeral costs for, in her own words, 'when the time comes'. They reluctantly agreed. Upon entering the funeral parlour, nan was shown a range of items she could choose from and pre-pay for. After about 20 minutes, a staff member approached the three of them and asked if they had chosen what they needed.

Nan was easily confused and asked for more time. Then the funeral director asked if she would like a cup of tea. My nan replied, 'Yes, I think I will because I won't get offered one next time I visit.' The funeral director appeared dumbfounded, looked towards my mother and aunty and said, 'I've never heard that one before!' My dear old nan made a common sense and sound risk assessment without ever knowing it. Legally, staff are obliged to assess foreseeable risks and make a plan to reduce them; otherwise, staff may be accused of negligence. No staff member should be expected to eliminate all risk. The aim is to attempt to reduce risks within the setting in which the child is. If I were to be flippant, the only way to eradicate all risk in a setting is to not invite any children into the building and then not invite staff in either – and we then might just about have zero risk. Of course, we are not lucky enough to work under those circumstances, so there will be some risk and the risks that are naturally there will increase or decrease depending on a variety of circumstances.

I have four children. As much as I want to believe I will always keep them safe, in reality this is not possible. For instance, they are not always in my care, and even when they are, they still have accidents and near misses. I once lost my eldest son for a whole 5 minutes whilst walking through my local town centre. There were three roads nearby and I was beside myself shouting his name and asking passersby if they had seen a young boy. Eventually I saw him hiding behind a wall with a big smile on his face (little monkey). The best I can do is act in good faith when taking care of my own children and trust that others will do the same and try to reduce the risk to the minimum possible.

If the risk is unknown, it is impossible to complete a planned risk assessment. Some children with ASD are unpredictable. Their behaviour is easily influenced by events and people outside their school environment. It is not possible to predict a child's behaviour or responses on every occasion. Sometimes I see a child engage in unsafe behaviour which had not been anticipated and I have to make a dynamic risk assessment. I have to make an important and difficult decision there and then. Can I de-escalate the behaviour? Do I have to consider using a physical intervention whilst continuing to de-escalate? After I have made the dynamic risk assessment, I would need to consider a planned risk assessment for the future as the risk had become known or anticipated.

I once received a phone call from a primary school to demonstrate to a group of staff how to disarm a child who had been using a cricket bat to cause damage to property and, more alarmingly, had hurt four members of staff. The boy had smashed the physical education (PE) store room with the bat, put large dents in the plaster and hit the door many times. This was a high-risk situation; staff had suffered injuries. When I visited the school, I could tell several of the staff were still upset about the incident and were concerned it might happen again. The school wanted me to train staff to remove the bat from the child. I spent over an hour talking to them about how they could make sure he didn't access the bat in the first place. They were insistent about learning how to physically disarm the child, which I felt was missing the point of it all. The PE store room had been unlocked and there was no key to lock it. My suggestion was to lock the PE store room and, for an added safety measure, use a bolt at the top of the door to stop any child from accessing the equipment without consent. No, staff still wanted to practise disarming the child with the bat. My feeling was this: prevention is better than cure. If he hadn't had the bat in the first place, he couldn't have used it to hurt people and cause damage to property. This was the most effective planned risk assessment conclusion after knowing what the child was capable of.

I went through the whole incident and encouraged them to replay it in their minds. Their thinking was to relive the fear, and then they became stuck at the end result – staff hurt and property damage. Let us rewind the incident and make a planned risk assessment in case this were to happen again:

- The store room is locked, which means no access to equipment which could be used as weapons.

- Give less risky sports equipment such as sponge footballs.

- Remove the audience.

When the child was in the room hitting the walls and door, staff needed to stay outside that room. It required only two staff members to stay nearby and observe, and the other staff should have left.

Property can generally be repaired or replaced, humans cannot. If staff keep their distance and stay assertive whilst communicating positive ideas, there is a fair chance the situation will come to an end. Of course, staff also need to evaluate why the incident occurred and if the triggers could have been avoided beforehand.

I am convinced with this incident that if staff had removed the audience and stayed away from the cupboard, waited for the child to burn himself out, talked and listened and starved him of any unnecessary attention, the child would have presented less risk to the staff. What happened is that the staff fed the child's behaviour and the boy's mind became highly aroused and stimulated. It was certainly not easy for staff is this situation. As staff we can stabilise a situation and make it safer by making dynamic risk assessments and then considering options to reduce the risk.

Planned risk assessments

I received a phone call from a primary school regarding a 5-year-old boy. The staff were concerned because they were having to manage unsafe behaviours including deliberately running into staff and children, absconding from school and hitting staff. The adults in the school were worried about intervening and wondering how best to protect themselves and other children.

To get to this stage of reasonable thinking, the staff must have made a dynamic risk assessment of the child's behaviour and wanted support to draw up a planned risk assessment. Calculating foreseeable risks can support staff to sequence and predict what could happen next. Risk assessments are similar to flow charts where there are different points to consider and options from which to choose. There are five steps to making a risk assessment:

1.   Identify the *hazard*.

2.   Decide who might be harmed and how.

3.   Evaluate the risk and decide on the *necessary* and *proportionate* action.

4.   Record your findings.

5.   Review and revise findings (if necessary).

This is a common sense checklist to follow and will be helpful in any incident or circumstance.

The key words involved in these five steps are *hazard, necessary* and *proportionate*. A hazard can be anything that could cause harm or make a person or the environment unsafe. The worst hazard I have experienced in a school was a chair made from lightweight plastic with metal legs that acted like four spears as it thrust towards me. It was a chair that is commonly found in many settings. They make fantastic missiles too, as they bounce around uncontrollably. Heavier chairs with padded seats and wider-shaped legs would be less of a hazard because they would be harder to pick up in the first place and would travel with less speed over a shorter distance.

Guidance

Generally, guidance assists people in setting standards. Guidance is usually written by organisations to provide advice to their members. For example, the Health and Safety Executive (HSE) in the UK provides guidance on a range of topics including risk assessments and manual handling or lifting. This would be helpful and necessary for baggage handlers in airports, for example. My mother's suitcase always gets one of those red stickers depicting a person holding their back in pain with the words 'HEAVY LOAD' stamped on it. My father always complains, 'How does your case weigh so much when I have most of your clothes in my case?' This is a moot point. In theory, guidance helps to protect employers by describing best practice and what is considered safe practice. Some guidance refers to legislation and regulations. The HSE guidance on manual handling or lifting suggests people refer to the Manual Handling Operations Regulations of 1992 (HSE 2004) to find information. Employers and organisations have an obligation to follow this legislation. The majority of employers may not realise this unless they read the guidance. I suggest that guidance does what it says on the tin: guide us to what we need to be doing to keep ourselves and others safe. This does not always mean that it makes our jobs easier, just safer. For instance, it would probably be quick and easy to lean over and pick something up off the floor and place it on a high shelf out of the way. But what if the box is very heavy and an awkward shape? Next consider that the high shelf is a good distance above head height and a mechanical devise should be used to help with this task. Following the guidance would reduce the risk of injury in this case. Training also comes into play. The UK Special Educational Needs and Disability Code of Practice 0–25 years (DfE/DoH 2014) highlights the need for appropriate training and positive handling to prevent injury or damage to property. It also points out the importance of having a written plan agreed and signed by parents and, if possible, the child. Training delivered by experienced professionals can give support to others on how to implement the guidance and legislation in our work practice. Behaviour management runs on the same set of principles. There is typically more than one approach to think about and many ideas to consider when trying to problem solve.

What many people find when reading through workplace and practice guidance is that often there are no clear, definitive answers or solutions – just information *guiding* us on the best path to follow. I suppose this is preferable to dictated notions that staff must follow to the letter. There are no known courses that teach staff to lift children unless it is an emergency. What defines an emergency is open to interpretation. What about if there was a fire in a building and a child was refusing to cooperate or was frozen with fear? Do staff follow the guidance and never pick a child up? How do we explain that a staff member left a child in a burning building because he or she had been instructed never to lift a child? Common sense and risk assessments have to be considered and followed. That is why I stated at the start of this chapter that all three factors (risk assessments, guidance and legalities) overlap and blend together.

If government guidance is statutory, it has greater legal force. One of the issues with guidance is that it can be non-statutory. This means that the guidance would have no jurisdiction in a court of law. A judge could say, 'That is merely guidance; it is up to this court to decide if the individual has given the paramount consideration to the child and acted in the child's best interests'. Some guidance *is* statutory, but sometimes I read through guidance of this nature and think it can be more harmful to the staff that is intending to help. Guidance can be written by people who do not work in the profession on which they are advising (e.g. politicians). I personally would stick very closely to legislation in your state or country to which the state or national legal system will ultimately adhere. After all, it is up to the courts to decide if a staff member has acted reasonably in the circumstances when put under the microscope.

Training

Currently, 19 of 50 states in the US do not have any statutory requirements regarding the use of restraints and seclusion practices in schools. Guidance is provided through taskforce recommendations. Other states have varying requirements of different degrees; their guidance may be either broad or detailed in its design. There is a general flavour to all of the guidance which suggests that staff need to follow certain procedures, such as trying not to use excessive force, and use behaviour plans when considering the use of medical, mechanical and manual restraint. Nearly all states advocate that staff need to access approved training, preferably *before* they restrain a child.

An example of this sentiment can be taken from State New Mexico's 'Use of Physical Restraint as a Behavioural Intervention for Students with Disabilities' (2006), which states:

> We recognize that there may be certain instances where manual restraint of a student may be necessary, so the remainder of this guidance addresses its appropriate use for students with disabilities.

It goes on to state:

> Any staff or staff team designated to apply physical restraint must be professionally trained and/or certified in the particular technique being used. This must happen *prior to* any such procedures being used on a student. Staff chosen to be trained to apply physical restraint should be individuals who are physically able to do so and can handle a crisis in a calm manner [emphasis as original].

This is not a legal requirement for staff in settings that children access to receive training. I feel that staff need to speak up and request training in de-escalation and physical intervention and then retain their accreditation by attending refresher courses. This would be a safe measure that would protect both staff and children.

Legalities

Here are just some of the difficult questions I have been asked time after time:

- 'Is it okay if I pick a child up?'

- 'Can I stop a child from running away?'

- 'How do you stop a child from kicking you?' (Move out of the way would be a start for that one!)

I am not being intolerant. There is sometimes a level of uncertainty and confusion that causes people to raise these queries. It is often due to fear that in retrospect staff have reacted in a manner about which they are now concerned. Children with ASD usually reach high levels of anxiety when in challenging situations, which further complicates the issues. The quick answer to any similar questions is that as professional adults working with children, we are by law not allowed to touch, hold, move or contain a child. This is based on common law that most countries incorporate into their legal system. My experience is that the vast majority of staff in social care and educational settings need the legal standing on physical intervention clarified. I feel that if staff actually had more of an understanding of how the law operates, there would be less restraint and more thought given to de-escalation and placement. I will always argue profusely that using legal and medically sanctioned holds and restraint techniques can support children in their settings. Sometimes holding or guiding a child with ASD or any other condition can help to de-escalate their behaviour; however, this is not a reason to administer these techniques, as they are more of an intervention that is implemented as the final strategy. I have worked with countless children who would have been excluded from their setting if staff could not physically intervene regularly. Personally, I have used physical intervention to prevent injuries to myself and other staff. Legally, staff that become injured could complain and seek financial compensation. Staff have a legal right to defend themselves and use reasonable actions to prevent themselves from becoming harmed in any way. I have never said, 'I do not come to work to be hurt by children or abused'. I have always thought of this type of sentiment as a no-brainer. Who does go to work and wants to get injured? No one in their right mind would want that. (Even professional boxers or police officers know that there is a substantial risk and they still hope to be okay when faced with the risks.) I believe we go through our working life by the grace of God and I would rather staff accept that there is a risk and be prepared to calculate the risk to help reduce it. It is important, however, to evaluate why a child's behaviour escalated to such a degree that a hold was necessary and plan future steps to try to prevent it being needed in the future.

The figures for staff facing aggressive behaviour from children in general are quite staggering. In the UK the Department for Education (2013) revealed that 4100 children are excluded for different fixed periods of time every week in British schools. This prompted some staff to call for the wearing of shin pads to protect themselves from being kicked. This is the wrong way of thinking. It is reactive, not proactive. Staff often reflect on their practice and worry that they did not react in the best way. Staff need to think about their de-escalation and communication skills, which will always be their frontline defence, and then access training on physical intervention. Children with special education needs are 10 to 11 times more likely to be excluded from UK schools. My own experience is that children with ASD are usually at far greater risk of exclusion for behavioural concerns. The US Indicators of Crime and Safety (Robers *et al.* 2014) reported that during 2011–2012 10 per cent of public school teachers were threatened with injury and 6 per cent were physically attacked by students. The percentage of elementary teachers who reported being physically attacked was 8 per cent compared with 3 per cent of secondary teachers.

Legal defence

Aggressive, violent and difficult behaviours go on in settings all over the world, and staff, like it or not, have to think through these possibilities very carefully and be aware of the option they have of using force to physically intervene and how they need to try to stay within the legal requirements. This requirement is that adults supporting children of any age located within any provision use *reasonable* force when it is *necessary* and *proportionate*. Three key words to take note of are:

- *Reasonable.* Was the force used reasonable in all the circumstances?

- *Necessary.* Was the use of force necessary in the circumstances or, simply put, was there a need for any force at all?

- *Proportionate.* Was the amount of force used fair in the circumstances?

EXAMPLES OF USE OF FORCE

Below are two examples of how force can be used in different contexts and still be deemed reasonable, necessary and proportionate.

Example 1

A 15-year-old girl with severe learning difficulties and ASD is walking to a café to practise life skills using the Picture Exchange Communication system. She has no traffic awareness and a member of staff holds her hand, which in the past has been an effective way of keeping her safe. She has never protested about this and enjoys the trip to the café. On one occasion she breaks free of the adult's hand and runs into a busy road and then stands in the middle of the road whilst several cars drive past. Within 5 seconds a colleague steps in the road to stop the traffic while I run into the road, grab the girl by her coat and pull her back onto the pavement.

Example 2

A 15-year-old boy with Asperger's syndrome is directed to leave a gym in a school because of a confrontation that happened during a game of soccer with four other teenagers. He leaves by himself without any physical intervention. Several minutes later, he walks back towards the gym and tries to regain entry. The member of staff asks him to wait outside, but he resists and tries to push his way back into the gym. The member of staff instructs him to stay outside and he pushes the staff member backwards several times. I approach the member of staff and ask him if he needs help. He asks me to open the doors behind me in the corridor and he then (using a recognised technique from an accredited course) guides the boy into the corridor and away from the other children. Later, the member of staff explains to me that the boy wanted to re-enter the gym to fight another child and, after guiding him away, he was held for 3 minutes in a two-person standing hold. He was then released and given the option of going outside for some fresh air, which he chose to do, and later returned into school without further difficulty.

Both of these examples achieved the same outcome for the child. In example 1 the physical contact made was an emergency response following a dynamic risk assessment, and in example 2 an approved restrictive physical intervention (RPI) was used. Both children were moved from one place to another to promote safety. Both children were moved because it was in their best interest. This is the paramount consideration for adults to take into account. In example 1 it was clearly in the best interests of the child to be removed from the centre of the road because of the high risk of being hit by a car. Factor in that the child had little knowledge of road safety and had learning difficulties; therefore, this action was necessary, reasonable in the circumstances and proportionate because of the high risk. In example 2 it was not in the child's best interest to re-enter the gym because his intention was to fight with one or more of the students. Fights are high risk, especially at that age, and high risk for staff to separate safely. The guiding away to another area is considered a low-level RPI. The next RPI was used because the risk increased and was a restraint implemented by two members of staff to prevent the young person from returning to the gym to fight. This action was necessary and proportionate, and the risk was calculated during the incident. As soon as the young person was displaying signs of being back in control, the intervention stopped and he was offered an option that would continue to reduce his challenging behaviour and improve the overall situation.

Neither of these incidents was pleasant or what I went to work that day to do. My colleagues and I made dynamic risk assessments and acted in good faith to ensure the safety of the children. After both of these incidents, planned risk assessments were made and shared with key staff in order to reduce the likelihood of the behaviour re-occurring.

Another sound legal defence is to consider, *If that had been my own child, I would have done exactly the same thing.* This is reasonable thinking because for me it is the same whether I am taking care of my own children or those of someone else. I have an equal duty of care to keep every child I come into contact with safe, spot foreseeable risks and act in a proportionate and reasonable manner.

Common law

In most countries, the legal system operates to give significant weight to what is usually referred to as the 'common law'. This is law developed by judges through the court system and works on the principle that it would be unfair to consider similar facts differently on different occasions. Common law is there to protect everyone from being hurt by other people. Common law is established in most countries around the world including every state in the US. No one has the absolute right to touch, hold or contain another person. Lots of staff do not realise that they have no powers or authority to do what they feel they should or want to do. This has a sound basis because otherwise any adult could make physical contact with a child without any justification. There are several important words that can help guide staff when using force to keep children and adults safe. Let us not run away from the fact that staff sometimes have to apply force when physically touching to reassure, guide, hold or restrain.

A physical intervention using reasonable force is likely to be defensible if the adult is trying to:

- prevent children from hurting themselves

- prevent injury to the child, other children, adults, parents or visitors in a setting

- prevent damage to property

- prevent a criminal act.

While I would emphasise that *any* 'physical' intervention to execute the tasks above has to be reasonable, necessary and proportionate, what responsible parent or carer would not want their child to be kept as safe as possible when all other possibilities have been considered?

Duty of care

If in common law staff that support and educate children do not have powers and authority to touch, hold, move or contain a child, it may be that their duty of care enables them to do so. Countries have their own legislation to consider if and when a duty of care is needed and by whom. In the UK the courts use the Children Act (1989) which states that 'the child's welfare shall be the court's paramount consideration'. This is directly linked to how the adults considered the 'best interests of the child' when a court determines any question with respect to the safety of the child and the actions of others. Canadian and New Zealand law mention that a duty of care is a legal obligation which is imposed on an individual requiring a reasonable standard of care to prevent foreseeable risk (Kemp and Merkelbach 2011). In the education and care context, *duty of care* is a common law concept that refers to the responsibility of staff to provide children and young people with an adequate level of protection against harm (South Australian Legislation 2011). In Australia each state will clarify what 'duty of care' means and how it impacts on the staff member's decision making.

In the US it is up to individual states to use their legislation to determine if the defendant's actions match with the standard of a reasonable person. A 'reasonable person' is defined as how a reasonable person would act in similar circumstances. Failing to act reasonably and not attempting to follow a duty of care could result in being proven negligent. It is worth remembering that the law on duty of care has gone through a number of changes over many years and is open to interpretation. Alexander and Alexander (2011) mention that in determining whether a duty of care exists, a court must first consider the foreseeable risks to the child who is placed within the care of the adult. This is fundamental to the actions that are later interpreted by the reasonable adult. I was reminded of this quite recently in my job. A lawyer said to me, 'It is not down to you to consider whether the way you acted was in the best interests of the child and whether you followed your duty of care, it is the responsibility of the court to decide.' This is sobering and true advice that is helpful because it keeps us thoughtful and honest.

KEY POINTS

- Staff need to consider their best and most robust legal defence: their paramount consideration of caring for the child.

- Use dynamic and planned risk assessments when de-escalating and before using physical interventions or positive handling techniques.

- Staff need to follow their duty of care and think about what is in the best interests of the child or young person.

CHAPTER 8

Restrictive Physical Intervention and Positive Handling

In 2011, *The Guardian* reported that the UK Education Minister, Michael Gove, wanted education staff to feel confident and competent when dealing with challenging children (Vasagar 2011). I'm sure any government in the world would like the same. The British Institute of Learning Disabilities (BILD) (2010) states that professionals who have a duty of care should seek to use, when necessary and reasonable, positive handling interventions to safeguard children. Since the mid-1990s, more children with challenging behaviours have been included in mainstream settings than ever before (Wolfendale and Robinson 2006). In mainstream settings, children with autism are included in most, if not all, curriculum activities. Emerson *et al.* (2001) maintain that 10–15 per cent of children with disabilities display behaviours which present a significant challenge to adults and settings. This not only impacts on the staff's time at school but can have an impact on other children's learning.

The DFE (2010) reports that the issue of physical restraint has been taboo and the lack of guidance and research has been damaging. Leadbetter (2002) explains that there has been a historical vacuum of research on safe, legally defensible approaches to restraint. Allen (2001) and Brown (2012) found that there has been very little research into the use of physical interventions in mainstream settings. Emerson (2002) and Allen (2001) think that this is because there is reluctance by governments to fund research which may prove controversial. Instead, the vast majority of research regarding the use of restraint has been in perceived 'higher-risk environments' such as psychiatric hospitals, special schools, remand units and prisons. This is despite the rise over the past 15 years in the inclusion of children with special educational needs into mainstream settings.

Butler's law: spare the rod, spoil the child

I grew up with my parents and many other adults in the area I was born preaching Butler's law. It always incensed me that some adults would try to follow the logic of this statement. Samuel Butler was not the original author of this sentiment. In 1663, Butler wrote the 'Hudibras', a poem satirising the English Civil War, especially the Puritans. As is so often the case, the true meaning of the saying is debatable. Physical punishment, chastising and intimidation were the norm until relatively recently. Corporal punishment was not banished from UK schools until 1986 (the year I left secondary education). I can remember the same students time and time again lining up outside the deputy head teacher's office waiting for their turn to receive the strap. In the US there are 19 states that still technically allow corporal punishment, although in practice it is becoming less common. Restrictive physical interventions (RPI) are far removed from the days of physically hurting a child to teach them a behavioural lesson. RPI need to be about keeping the child and others safe.

Restraint has had a bad reputation in the past due to previous inferior practice in several industries, confused messages from governments and local authorities, poor and sometimes misleading guidance and then some staff who openly abused children by using unlawful restraint techniques. During the 1980s–1990s, restraint became a taboo subject, a 'dirty word' where adults hurt children by administering various locks and holds to justify their means. I experienced what I would define as unhelpful and inappropriate restraint techniques over 20 years ago.

I worked on a summer camp for two summers in New York State in the early 1990s. I loved the experience of working in another country, meeting American children and engaging them in a vast range of outdoor activities. I was initially employed for the summer as a karate instructor amongst other things. Once I got there and started to settle in, I quickly realised that the management team were very apprehensive about showing children between the ages of 5 and 16 years any form of martial arts in case they used it in an inappropriate way. I could understand why they thought this, particularly because the children were from very deprived areas of Long Island, New Jersey and New York City. It could be argued that some kids from Patterson (New Jersey) or the South Bronx didn't need any further tuition from a karate instructor! However, I was an experienced instructor and knew what to show and what values and discipline to try to instil. I was allowed to take a small group of senior campers for five sessions. Despite my disappointment that after having travelled a long distance I couldn't use the skills that I had originally been asked to deploy, I didn't push for other children to be included.

During my time at the camp, much to my amazement and shock I witnessed a restraint called 'decking'. All the counsellors were informed that this was a legal technique in New York State at that time but could only be implemented by those adults who had received training. Decking basically consisted of forcing the child onto the floor in a prone position and then sitting on their back whilst holding onto various limbs that might be 'causing problems'. The first time I witnessed this I felt sick (as did others who were unfamiliar with the technique). Some counsellors were in tears. My first impression was that it was totally over the top despite appearing effective. Children would often scream, shout or cry. Then they would submit usually while listening to the adult talk about who was the boss. There was little time for positive listening and debriefing. It was based on punishment. It was, of course, totally inappropriate, unnecessary and unreasonable. I was surprised that more children did not get seriously hurt. I can still conjure up the vision of the children with a terrified expression in their eyes. Basket holds were also used. (Basket holds have been greatly discouraged by the BILD in the UK, because this restraint involves placing the child's arms across their chest and pulling their hands behind or to the side of their body.) Any restraint that holds across the upper body and on the chest restricts breathing. This has to be avoided, obviously. Breathing and circulation need to remain unaffected. In the late

1990s I attempted to use this hold and was injured every time. This is because the child can throw their head directly backwards towards the adult and the head then makes contact with the adult's chest area or face.

There has been some rethinking over the past few years about which techniques are safest. I feel there will always be a need for reflecting on how the biomechanics work and striking a balance between having a method that is effective and supportive. Just because the method works well does not make it safe or reassuring for both adult and child. Sitting on a child that has been 'decked' or grabbing a child's arm and placing it behind their back may be effective but is morally and ethically wrong, in my opinion.

In Staffordshire (UK) there was the infamous 'pin down'. This was an approach used in some care homes where children were often placed in rooms for weeks without appropriate clothing and furnishings and subjected to various punishments such as beatings, pain-compliance restraint techniques and being given remedial tasks such as copying from telephone books. An inquiry into the practice was undertaken by Allan Levy QC in 1990–1991. Clearly, we all need to be very careful and transparent when using RPIs and consider holding or restraining a child only as a last resort. Each individual setting needs to have a policy on physical intervention that promotes the staff duty of care and use of de-escalation strategies as well as including how to make risk assessments as well as record and report incidents appropriately. This would go a long way in making sure staff use accredited and safe techniques that protect children from harm and allow a degree of movement, clarifying that there is no intention to punish – just to safeguard and protect the child.

I often read on websites and in books written on the subject of RPIs that there are no accredited courses available. In the UK the BILD awards accreditation to a number of training providers. In my own experience, it is worth exploring these training providers first, due to the fact that they have been accredited by BILD, to find out what sort of backup support and advice they provide following the training course. It is a good idea to find out from these providers if legal and medical experts have examined the RPI and positive handling techniques that are included on their training courses. In 2009, the then US Secretary of Education sent a letter to the

Chief State Schools Officers stating that she was 'deeply troubled' about the current use and effects of restraint (US Department of Education 2009, p.155). One of the biggest concerns was that there were no current federal regulations; instead, there was a wide variety of state regulations regarding the topic of restraint. The US Department of Education was calling for a number of changes and review of policies and procedures. In 2014, the US Senate issued a report on the 'Dangerous Use of Seclusion and Restraint in Schools' (US Senate HELP committee 2014). This report concluded that there were 66,000 cases of restraint or seclusion administered in schools. This wasn't the true picture because 15 per cent of school districts failed to supply data.

Many autistic children can end up on the receiving end of poor practice involving restraint, such as a young child who was placed in a duffel bag which was hung on a peg by his teacher. (He was found by his parent.) There are many training providers in the US that offer courses on conflict resolution, de-escalation and physical intervention, although it is unclear by what code of practice they are governed and sanctioned.

Choosing a provider

Learning Support Magazine reports that only one in three school staff have received any training on how to deal with potentially violent situations (Rickford 2010). Time has moved on and there are a number of courses available and specialised training that can and do provide safe, effective instruction for the vast majority of people. Many of the providers employ medical and legal experts to assess the techniques they advocate. Most of the providers try to emphasise de-escalation first and holding or restraint as the last resort. Unfortunately, there are courses that are designed to generate money first; they put course members at further risk, and the children are considered last. Furthermore, there is poor-quality training delivered by inadequate trainers. This is the case in any industry. Each country has a governmental department that accredits, or at least registers, organisations. I personally would research organisations that are accredited – but not exclusively, because I'm occasionally cynical and realise that government departments can make wrong decisions sometimes and may exclude organisations that may be competent.

As a trainer I have relied upon word of mouth. Most of my requests are from staff that say, 'I was given your number by…' or 'Another school recommended your training'. This is nice to hear. I certainly wouldn't get involved in money-making schemes or arrogant organisations that engage in slick websites and promise to solve all your problems or profess to know all the answers.

A useful way of choosing a competent and caring provider for training on de-escalation and physical intervention is to ask what they provide after the training has been done. If the response is that you can call for advice, that they will come back to refresh staff or offer further support for an agreed fee, that would generally be a positive sign they care about the quality of training that's provided.

Trainers may not realise how many staff and course members are full of nerves and very anxious when they attend training sessions that involve RPI. One of the jobs of the trainer is to settle nerves and reduce anxieties by clearly explaining the course content at the start. I know a colleague who attended a course and was confronted by three trainers dressed in black martial arts outfits! This is not a karate competition, folks. Most staff that make up the school population have some sort of nagging injury and this needs to be taken into consideration. How does the course provider look after your health and safety? Do they give you the option of observing and making your own risk assessments? I have lots of course members approach me when they first enter the training room and give me a list of aches and pains, details of operations and conditions from which they suffer. I always present the same advice: 'Please observe the demonstrations and then decide if you would like to practise with someone you trust and make your own risk assessment.' One particular course member approached me half-way through a course and said, 'I don't know whether I should be doing this. I have two metal plates in my head from a road traffic accident, had an aneurism in my leg and I once broke my neck.' He then asked, 'What do you think?' I replied, 'Wow, mate, you are a walking miracle. How are you still managing to stay alive?' He made his own risk assessment and joined in when *he* felt he could. That's the way it should be.

Pain compliance

Pain compliance is the application of a painful hold or technique for the purpose of controlling or directing a person. I am not in favour of using pain compliance when implementing RPIs. There may be an argument for the use of pain compliance in certain provisions or with certain children who are very strong or are large in stature. This is another level up from my experience, and although I have worked with children who are placed on the extreme end of the autism spectrum, I have only had to use techniques that are non-pain compliant. I am aware, however, that some professionals may depend upon and need techniques that rely on pain compliance. I do not subscribe to the thinking that those techniques only cause pain when the child offers a certain level of resistance. I have used Team Teach techniques that restrict a child's mobility. If they continue to struggle against the hold, I can apply more restriction by applying more force to keep the hold in place. Yes, there may be discomfort for the child – I will be standing or sitting very close – and yes, I might accidentally hold too tight. None of this is deliberate to cause any degree of discomfort or pain to the child. This would never be my intention. If I am trying to prevent a 'six-foot, thirteen stone child' from self-harming, then I may have to administer a very restrictive hold with another colleague. Do I want to do this in the first instance? No. Would I consider any other option? Yes. Would I then choose restraint in the best interests of that child? Probably yes. My thoughts will revert back to never have a 'never' in a policy or practice. If a child grabs a staff member's hair, twists and pulls with a lot of force and there is a risk this action will damage the person's neck, spine or head, I will use whichever technique I can at the time that will prevent serious injury by considering the best interests of the child and the staff member. With adrenalin flowing, the amount of force I apply may inflict pain or discomfort on the child which is a regrettable side effect of ensuring everyone remains safe. There is still a legal, ethical and moral obligation when considering the amount of force that would tip the RPI into pain compliance. I would hope that pain compliance would only be a response to a high-risk, emergency situation. Staff need to distinguish between deliberate pain-compliance techniques that are techniques learnt on training, and unintentional pain compliance which is due to the amount of force being applied to the child causing them to experience pain. These techniques need to be part of the child's risk assessment to qualify the reasons they are acting in the best interests of the child. Then, within the risk assessment, there needs to be information on how staff can reduce the likelihood of having to use techniques that involve pain compliance. This would then show staff intentions of moving towards using other non-pain-compliance RPIs.

Checklist for staff when considering physical intervention

I start most courses on de-escalation and positive handling by inviting course members to think about how they have felt or would feel if they were faced with the prospect of holding a child to maintain their own and the child's safety. I often witness the look of horror on their faces. Some course members looked pained as they recall the last occasion they were involved in a physical intervention. This is how I would expect and want staff to react. I would be in deeper trouble and far more concerned if staff on courses were telling me how much they enjoyed the last time it happened and look forward to the next! The important question on everyone's lips is, 'How do I know when it is right to physically intervene?'

I feel that it is not a matter of right and wrong. The pressure of trying to decipher whether I need to physically intervene or not can be immense, and it's a decision I may not get right. I would prefer to think, *What is the better option? How can I make this safer?* For me it is not about the adult doing a test with a pass or fail. This is an extraordinary decision a person has to make in their career and one most would prefer not to have to make.

There is a four-point checklist I use to great effect:

1. Is the action the adult has chosen necessary?

2. Is the staff member acting reasonably?

3. Is the action chosen proportionate?

4. Is the action chosen in the best interests of the child?

This is a robust and useful checklist. It provokes serious thought into the action the adult is taking. It is reliable enough if staff think *yes* to all of the four points and equally reliable if staff think, *No, it is not in the best interests of the child* or *It is not necessary yet.* This checklist assists staff to make the best informed decision on behalf of the child. It is still the staff member's decision and they can choose not to physically intervene. For example: A staff member is concerned about a girl receiving an injury because she has limited communication and throughout the day she regularly slaps her face and punches her body. She also falls on the floor face down and headbutts the floor. I have to state that if this was my child, I would want a member of staff to try to prevent her from causing injury to her face and head. It would be in her best interests not to self-harm. For staff to follow their duty of care, they need to work in the best interests of the children they support and the paramount consideration is the child's welfare. Staff are not fitted with a GPS system to be guided through a situation; we are human with human responses. This is extremely difficult work. Let us make no bones about that; however, it is a realistic proposition for many staff and one they will have to contemplate from time to time. My experience over the past 5 years is that staff in general are more interested in avoiding restraint than administering it. This is not to say that some staff have poor judgement, take risks or think they can do what they like.

Whenever a staff member considers using physical contact with a child, they need to consider the force required. The force applied needs to be reasonable and proportionate to the situation. When there is an issue of holding children or physically intervening, staff need to think clearly what their intention is. There needs to be a *gradual-and-graded* approach to physical intervention. This is not a black-or-white situation – it's one hell of a big grey area! Let us explore the options adults have when using force to influence a child's behaviour.

The use of force has to be *proportional.* There's no need to split a walnut with a sledge hammer. Here is a sliding scale of use of force to physically intervene:

1. guide

2. escort

3. hold

4. restraint standing or in seated position

5. restraint on the ground

6. restraint in prone or supine position.

My observations in some settings I have visited or worked in over the years is that staff can fall into a habit of holding children without considering the alternatives. This may be shocking to outsiders who have never experienced the challenges of working with children diagnosed on the spectrum. Some parents may become horrified and incensed that their child is repeatedly held by staff in their setting. I empathise with both sides equally. I have never liked holding a child even though it was to keep them safe or to reduce the risks involved. It is an unpleasant course of action with concerning consequences to contemplate. There have probably been excessive physical interventions in lots of service settings. There are several reasons for this such as lack of training, or training that has too much emphasis on RPI and too little on communication and de-escalation.

Emotional vs physical response from the adult

After ten years of using an established and respected training provider's RPI techniques, I realised I had missed a trick. From the very first course I attended in 2000, I had always been concerned I would get hurt when attempting an RPI, when actually there is another part to consider. No staff should enjoy holding or restraining a child. If staff are relishing the idea of going to work to hold children, then we are all in trouble. My own feelings of making a decision to hold a child are often those of dread and trepidation.

Here is a list of comments about feelings experienced by course members when they have physically intervened with a child:

- start sweating and feel sick

- nervous, worried and unsure

- frightened

- scared I'm not doing the right thing

- scared I'm going to hurt the child

- worried that I may not be doing the hold in the right way

- concerned that what I'm doing may not be legal and safe

- worried that I may not be okay to do this

- worried that I may get in trouble

- concerned about possibly hurting the child.

This is a fine list of doubts from staff that care about the children with whom they work. The examples from this list show normal levels of uncertainty that any reasonable adult would need to demonstrate. One of the aims of training in de-escalation and positive handling strategies is to improve staff confidence levels so they can make informed decisions. It is interesting to note that the adults are more concerned with the welfare of the child and implementing the safest response than they are of protecting themselves. The picture that is being painted is of how staff can protect children. During over 350 training sessions on de-escalation and physical intervention, I have rarely heard staff say that they worry about getting hurt themselves. This is evidence to me that training and support for staff who are working with children with challenging behaviour is vitally important. In every school, within every setting where there are children who may become aggressive, upset and challenge, staff need to be able to exercise their option of physical intervention as a last resort to attempt to keep children, young people and themselves safe.

My own experience is similar. I have always recognised RPI as a necessity of looking after and taking care of the child's welfare. I do not mind admitting that I have sometimes dreaded driving to work knowing that I would probably have to implement an RPI.

I have occasionally trodden on eggshells knowing that saying the wrong thing or responding in a certain way would ignite a child's aggression and cause the need for an RPI. This is never a good place to find yourself. Having to make important decisions about the implementation of an RPI is very stressful. There is usually a massive degree of pressure involved. How staff manage the pressure usually determines the outcomes of how children behave and certainly how they react. Staff dealing with children who have autism spectrum disorder (ASD) need to assert confidence. Children with ASD can have lots of anxieties that manifest as challenging behaviours. Most children with ASD that I have supported appear to look towards the adults to apply safe boundaries and interventions. When this doesn't happen, I feel children become more volatile and their anxiety manifests in behaviours that become difficult to manage.

As an industry we are more aware of the risks involved and the feelings of both the children and the adults when using RPI. In services and organisations that provide care or education for children, there is more consideration about de-escalating situations first and only then trying to use any form of physical intervention as a last resort; however, there are still organisations that over-highlight physical intervention above all else. Training that involves RPI should have a balance ratio of at least 60 per cent to 40 per cent in favour of de-escalation. The emphasis needs to be on how RPI should be implemented only as a last resort. What does last resort mean? In the context of teaching staff how to guide or hold safely, last resort in my practice means to exhaust all other options before a decision is made to physically intervene.

'To hold or not to hold?' That is the question!

How does the adult qualify their decision to physically intervene? First things first: never have a policy that has the words 'never' or 'always' in it. It's dangerous and unfair to direct any staff member to physically intervene or instruct them that they should never do so. Every situation is different, and using absolutes can place children and adults in greater jeopardy.

Staff can sometimes fall into two categories: those who rush into holding and those who run a mile. I have never understood why some staff feel the need to keep intervening and moving very close to the child. Is it the need to feel dominant and in control? Maybe it is, and it really drives me mad! If a child is safe sitting by themselves on the floor, lying on the carpet or pacing up and down, and they are not hurting themselves or another person, then let's back off and leave them alone. Why is there this incessant need to keep getting close and make physical contact? This is a criticism because I have witnessed too many staff get hurt and children who become more aggressive as a result. It's actually a fundamentally basic strategy to back off and observe from a distance. It may look like the adult is not doing anything, but they are.

Children are like boiling kettles. When a kettle has been boiled, it is hot and therefore dangerous; so is the child when they overheat. The kettle takes a long time to cool down and for the water to be a safe temperature. The kettle appears safe when there is no visible steam; however, appearances can catch us out. This presumption can apply to the child. They can take a while to cool down and be safe to approach. They might appear calm on the outside but still be quite agitated. This kind of experience can apply to children being held. They may struggle against the RPI to begin with and then start to become calmer in their body language, tone of voice and verbal communication. This does not always come naturally and needs to be practised. The adult in this situation has to grin and bear it and try to keep modelling positive non-verbal and verbal communication.

I think that sometimes staff feel that the use of restraint will solve all their problems. During a 1-day training session at a primary school, I was approached by a staff member who asked me to show her an RPI technique to force a child back into the classroom. (I did think straight away that usually staff consider how to *remove* the child from the classroom, not try to get them back in!) Non-verbal communication, such as body language, can often give away people's intentions when asking questions like this. The manner in which staff ask questions informs me of their real intentions, and I felt at the time that this staff member was missing the point. I considered that there is no specific technique for getting a child to return to the classroom, and legally we have no right to hold or contain another person unless it is in their best interests. Taking a resentful and aggressive child back into a classroom with 30 other people does not seem like a great idea to me.

I asked her why there was a need to make this child go back into the classroom, and thus began our dialogue:

Staff member:	He needs to do his work like everyone else.
Me:	Can he do the work that's been set?
Staff member:	No.
Me:	Why not?
Staff member:	Well, it is too difficult for him.
Me:	Okay, do you differentiate the work for him?
Staff member:	No.
Me:	Why is there no differentiation?
Staff member:	We are told not to differentiate; all the children are given the same work.
Me:	Do you think that might be the problem?
Staff member:	It sounds very bad when I think about it now.

The staff member looked very embarrassed when she said this, and I left it at that. I walked away thinking I had been asked to show how to restrain a child who leaves the classroom because he is being presented with work that is too difficult. I suppose the staff working with this child had got stuck thinking about what the end result was for themselves – 'How do we make the child work in the classroom?' – and had forgotten to start at the beginning and look at the reasons why the child was trying to escape in the first place. I feel this sort of scenario can present a negative and unnecessary view of restraint. On a de-escalation scale of 1–100, it is jumping to 100 without changing through the gears. Let us not use restraint as an easy and convenient option to change and challenge children's behaviour. If a child needs to be held or restrained, quantify why it was necessary, proportionate and reasonable. Is this an action that would be a last resort?

There is the concern that in any setting where there is a need for RPI, and the staff in the setting are trained in the use of RPIs, this could lead to becoming 'normal' practice. If de-escalation is ignored or practised poorly, RPIs become a quick and easy option and the human brain will take the path of least resistance. This is why after every RPI, I would encourage staff to reflect on what the child did and how staff responded.

I receive several phone calls per month that go along the lines of, 'You did some training a few months ago and we need you to visit and show us more restraint techniques because what we did on the training is not working'. I can honestly say that when I get this comment, I start thinking, *What they need is more de-escalation, not more RPI*. Often the technique needs tweaking to make it more effective, because staff often forget details following training if they do not use it straight away.

On one occasion I was asked to visit a primary school because a 7-year-old child was absconding out of the window of a room where he was either escorted to or went into of his own accord. There was a pop-up tent in the corner of the room for the child to hide away and have some quiet time. This strategy worked well but, like most strategies, not all of the time. When this boy refused to enter the tent or was too upset to listen, he would jump out of a ground-floor window. Sometimes he would lie on the window shelf on his stomach and balance like a see-saw. This behaviour was both upsetting and difficult to manage. It was physically unsafe for both staff and the child. What the staff asked for was a restraint technique to get the child back through the window. There isn't really a specific technique to use in this circumstance. This is an emergency situation and several issues need to be risk assessed. If an attempt is made to take the child back into the room, through the window, this could cause injuries to the child. If the child drops through the window onto the ground or stays on the window shelf, this could cause injuries as well – a dilemma for the staff especially if the child does hurt himself.

When I stood in front of the window pondering how I could help, I noticed that there was a rivet missing from the hinge that attached the locking device to the window. I continued to stare at the window and said, 'Could the window lock be fixed so he can't open the window in the first place?' The staff looked at me and exclaimed, 'That's a bloody good idea!' I was treated like a hero for the rest of the time I was there. I had made a simple risk assessment and had seen the problem with a fresh pair of eyes. This was the only advantage I had. I didn't know the child or school at all. I had kept the solution simple.

This certainly does not mean the staff didn't know what they were doing. The staff I met were doing an excellent job of supporting this child. They worked hard and cared about doing the best they could. The staff had missed the simplest solution because they had over-complicated the problem. They didn't need more RPI – it came down to risk assessment, more de-escalation and checking the environment. If I had been a staff member at that school, I would have missed the obvious because I wouldn't have seen the wood for the trees.

This state of affairs could be, and sometimes is, repeated in any setting. Why? Well, because as adults working under pressure and in stressful situations our brains can become dysfunctional. The brain can send panic messages and create confusion. I reckon similar cases to the example above account for 90 per cent more holding and restraint than is actually needed. RPI is an end product, that last resort when all else has failed or when a rapid response to a high-risk situation is needed. I have already stated my feelings that RPI can be a safe way of ensuring children are cared for and looked after. This doesn't mean it should be over-used or relied on as the only strategy.

More than the holding

Have a think about these next questions. In your job could you get through a day at work without making physical contact? Let's pretend you are not allowed to have any physical contact with children in your place of work. Could you do your job effectively and keep children safe?

Here are some situations when adults would need to have physical contact with children:

- administering first aid treatment

- shaking hands when greeting or congratulating

- helping a child who has fallen over get back on their feet

- giving high fives to express praise

- comforting a child who has become upset by placing an arm across the shoulders

- helping a child into a wheelchair or standing frame

- changing a child's pad or helping a child to toilet train

- accepting a young child's hand when they are scared or miss their family

- applying sun cream to prevent sunburn during outside play

- tying a child's shoe lace

- helping a child to climb over apparatus during a physical education lesson

- playing football

- feeding a child who cannot do this independently.

The list could go on and on. It is impossible for adults to work successfully and reasonably with a child of any age without them needing physical contact.

Arguments against restraining children

There are reasons why children should not be restrained. Some children are hypersensitive to touch or may have experienced sexual abuse, been physically hurt in previous restraints or lack the necessary capacity to communicate with the adults who are administering the restraint. There are some people who work with children or are in a non-professional capacity who feel that any restraint is ethically unacceptable, especially restraint in a prone position and using pain compliance. The feelings of various adults who naturally adopt a certain view (e.g. parents, foster carers, teachers, teaching assistants and care workers) need to be considered, but equally they need to see the dilemma from everyone's perspective. The issues that grind discussions to a halt is the lack of research done in this area, and counter discussions where some staff feel there are limited options when trying to support some individuals with ASD who are exceptionally strong and aggressive. They may feel there is no other alternative except to hold. It is all a grey area. So much depends on the staff member's capacity to de-escalate and manage the child's behaviour. Other factors to consider are the knowledge of the child, best methods of communication, personal or professional relationships, positive listening and debriefing.

The phrases 'restraining' and 'holding children' can send shivers down the spines of even the most experienced staff members. The thought of making a decision to physically intervene can be intimidating and frightening. When I ask staff in settings how they feel about the prospect of having to hold or how they felt when they did choose to hold or restrain a child, the answers I often receive are: scared, worried I might hurt them, vulnerable, uncomfortable, anxious and the question, 'Am I doing the right thing?' I can't ever recall anyone mentioning that they enjoyed the experience and would look forward to doing it again. Many of the course members state that another concern that enters their heads is whether they will get in trouble for physically intervening.

Out of necessity: physical contact and touch

I have supported children who have approached me and other staff members informing us that they need to be held or they will hurt someone. This may appear strange to people who have never worked alongside children with special educational needs and behavioural difficulties. If staff do not give certain children with ASD reassurance through physical touch, these children will continue to need restraining because the restraint will be the only time they will experience the comfort of being held by consistent and reasonable adults. No adult wants to restrain a child unless it is absolutely necessary. So let us rewind. If staff were to use physical contact as part of a planned and coordinated approach with certain children (obviously not children with ASD who are hypersensitive to touch), this would be helpful to reduce the number of restraints which can be more traumatic for both child and adult. This would reduce the risk of having to administer holds, prevent emotional stress and the likelihood of injuries. More importantly, staff can promote positive interactions which will create a safer working environment.

My autistic nephew, who is 13 years old, needs physical touch and always craves hugs. He sits close to people and leans on them. He feels safer and conveys his feelings about the person through this contact. He gets feedback from the physical touch and it helps him relate to other people. This is not too dissimilar to how children and adults without autism receive their feedback. If a person has not seen a family member or friend for a very long time, the hugs seem to be deeper and longer. If a friend or relative is going through a bad time, we might hug them or hold them and engage in a more meaningful conversation than normal. I admit this can be difficult for some people who are averse to touchy-feely interactions; however, we are considering children who may be vulnerable and need reassurance, so this is a professional approach that acts as a strategy. For those of us who are immediately thinking about child protection issues and increased allegations, let us think again! If there is a genuine need for physical contact, let's write it on the child's risk reduction or restraint reduction plan. Share it with everyone – parents and carers, staff and outside agencies. Write it into the setting policies. Make this the normal ethos of the setting.

This is not something staff do as an alternative approach. It is a strategy to keep children safe and reduce anxieties that can affect the child's learning and development. There are several children I am giving outside support and advice to at the moment where I am encouraging staff to use the same physical intervention prompt and guide when the child is doing well and is engaging positively as when they are needing the prompt or guide to keep them from trouble and keep them safe. I feel staff need to use physical touch as a matter-of-fact strategy when the child is going through a range of emotions so it becomes consistent, normal practice that reassures and supports emotional development. Some of these children, especially those with severe learning disabilities and others with limited communication, will experience negative interactions, so physical contact will be a positive connection with other people. Sanderson and Harrison (1991) explain that physical touch is a way of connecting, building a relationship and this encourages positive communication (p.11). Think about a stranger to whom you are introduced. Often a handshake is administered or a hand is offered to shake. If these two people speak different languages, it can help break down barriers and establish expectation and trust as well as build rapport.

I have worked with children who have actively sought an adult to hold or restrain them. It can place the adult in a very uncomfortable position. As adults we are trying to steer away from holding, so it can feel strange when children *want* to be held. My experience is that some children feel comfortable, safe and secure through close physical contact. Very often the adults receive verbal abuse and demands expressed aggressively. For example: 'Hold me or I'll hurt someone' or 'You better hold me now because I'm going to do something bad'. I have heard accounts where children become addicted to the restraint techniques and deliberately engage in unsafe behaviour which they know will lead to being held. I have never experienced this myself; it is rare but does happen.

When physical contact, such as guiding, firm squeezing across the shoulders with both hands, a friendly tap on the arm, arms across the shoulders and firm handshakes, is made throughout the day, it can help to avoid children ending up in restraints. The child is receiving the physical interaction he or she is seeking in an assertive and non-threatening manner. Children with ASD or those who are hyposensitive to touch can seek the feedback they crave or need to experience. This is about adults taking the initiative and pre-empting what the child may need. It is about the adults putting their own feelings to one side so the child can experience what she or he needs. This may come easier to some nationalities that show their emotions more often compared with people who are a little more reserved.

How many times have you experienced children trying to get your attention by tapping, prodding or leaning into you to show affection or because they are feeling tired? Perhaps in some way they are receiving feedback that is helping to satisfy a basic need.

Good vs bad touch

In recent years I have frequently given thought to children and young people who have been physically and sexually abused by adults or other children. I think about how tragic this must have been for those children who have had this most unfortunate experience in their life. Could some of these experiences have been avoided or stopped sooner if the children involved had familiarity with physical touch that was appropriate and in a safe context? If children could tell the difference between appropriate and inappropriate touch, maybe they could determine which adults are acting in good faith. I have noticed that in some special school settings or with very young children, or if the child's ASD makes them more innocent, gullible or compromises their communication, staff are more likely to think they can get away with more forceful physical contact that is unwarranted.

I have worked with children who have tragically been physically abused. I have first-hand knowledge about how it can destroy a child's life and have an effect on others around them. How many children over the past 50 years would have been able to either prevent being abused or realised that what an adult was doing or asking of them was wrong if they had been modelled what positive touch looked and felt like?

Positive holding and RPI techniques that are used with accredited organisations tend to focus on restricting movement of the arms and the adult standing sideways to the child. Private body parts, face, chest, back and upper legs are not held by the adult unless there is an emergency response where the child is going to cause serious harm. In my experience all the colleagues that have held onto body parts such as legs or head have usually done so through necessity or accident and stopped as soon as they possibly could.

Physical contact

The squeeze machine is not going to cure anybody, but it may help them relax; and a relaxed person will usually have better behaviour.

– Temple Grandin (1996)

Temple Grandin, a highly respected and famous adult with autism, talks openly about how physical touch can help to reassure children and people with ASD. She advocates deep-pressure touch because it can be relaxing and calming. This physical touch needs to be open and transparent, and it requires safety.

Physical contact with children is so important to foster trust and reassurance. Who can argue against an adult taking a child's hand that's been offered because the child is distraught at having to separate from his or her parents or placing an arm around the shoulders of a teenage girl because she is being bullied?

I often start my training sessions with the question, 'Can anybody in this room do their job safely and successfully without using physical touch with children?' Honestly, 100 per cent of course members shake their head and say no. I agree with them. I could not have done my job safely and successfully without using physical contact. Physical contact between children and adults is more frequent and less intense than restraint. Shaking hands, giving high fives, arm across shoulders and a pat on the shoulder are prime examples of physical contact – safe parts of the body to touch, well meaning, inoffensive and reassuring; of course, not for every person, but in my experience certainly the vast majority.

In the past 16 years of working with children with ASD and emotional, social and behavioural difficulties I have missed a trick. There were and are far more children than I first realised that needed physical touch to reassure and reinforce communication. As previously discussed, children with ASD can have sensory sensitivities. I will always respect children who do not like to be touched (appropriately) at any time. There is a greater issue at stake here and that is children with anxieties, emotional problems and those who are confused or frightened who need reassurance. Physical contact can be a strategy that provides that reassurance. Safe, open touch can promote confidence and provoke feelings that make most of us feel better. I feel settings could become safer, more pleasant places if staff used physical contact more often in a transparent and contingent way that sends positive reinforcement to auditory communication. Physical touch would complement the messages staff are giving when offering praise (e.g. shaking the child's hand at the same time of saying 'Well done!' or when asking if they are okay while placing a hand on their shoulder).

Timing

I have often heard practitioners in a variety of settings say that a child can be held only for 3 minutes (or a similar, specified amount of time.) This is, of course, total nonsense. There is no time limit to administer a hold or restraint. If there were a time limit of, let us say, 3 minutes and the child needed to be held for 5 minutes, what would be the point of releasing 2 minutes early? The factual evidence is that staff need to hold for as long as is reasonable and necessary. Staff need to look and listen to the child and continue to focus on de-escalation. The child will often say they are calm enough to be released when actually they aren't. Adults who know the child well can usually judge the timings well. A sound indicator of when to release the child from the restraint is when the risk is reduced and staff feel safer.

Furniture

It is important for staff to consider the safety aspect of the type of furniture the children can be held in to keep them safe. It is not the case that children are safer in a seated position, but it might be a preferred option. The seating arrangement needs to be comfortable, stable and at a suitable height. The greater the depth and the angle of recline, the better the chance of safe holding. If there is a large space between the seat and the floor (i.e. the length of the chair legs), the child can try to lever themselves forward and out of the seat. It is better to have a seating arrangement with less space between the seat and the floor.

The furniture needs to be strategically placed around the setting to avoid having to move the child too far. The seats need to have a multi-purpose use to avoid negative connotations such as the 'holding chairs'.

Unfair judgement

I recall that many years ago, I was questioned by a colleague as to why I had held a child. This colleague was insinuating I had acted hastily. I did not have any issue with the charge. There was no concern that this colleague was going to investigate the incident.

The problem I had was the method being used. My colleague was using hindsight. Yes, it can be a wonderful thing. If I could have had a second chance, I would have done things differently. I recognised I had not make the best choice. My defence was this: it was totally unfair for me to be criticised weeks after the incident by someone who was not placed in that position at that time. I'd had 10 seconds to make a risk assessment and then decide if an RPI was in the best interest of the child. My colleague needed to have placed herself in the same position – 10 seconds to make a decision, risk assess and react.

Let's place ourselves in other people's shoes when we try to understand their decision and the choice they made. This is the fairest way of approaching any staff member and questioning their practice. I held my hands up and said I would react differently if the child ever engaged in this behaviour again. When working under extreme pressure and where time is limited, it is always going to be difficult to make the best decision.

There are people and organisations that disagree with staff physically intervening. As already stated, in my opinion it is dangerous to have absolutes on this subject. For example, if a child in a school setting were to throw a chair across the room in anger and it hit another child and caused a serious injury, then reached for another chair to repeat the action, would it be reasonable to physically intervene to prevent further injury to others and further trouble for the perpetrator after several attempts of unsuccessfully using non-physical intervention?

Now put your own child in that position, close your eyes for 10 seconds and think how you would feel if none of the adults physically intervened to keep your son or daughter safe from harm. If you had a family member or your own child in the care of other professionals and they were at risk of being hurt by another child, would you expect the adults to protect him or her?

I feel it is necessary to have complete flexibility in policies and staff practice. If the message is that the setting has a 'no touch' policy (which means that staff must never physically intervene), it can place staff and children at risk during certain challenging situations. I have found myself in the most unpredictable circumstances where I never dreamed I would choose to escort or hold a child.

In Chapter 7, I referred to a student being removed from the road. My only concern was her safety and to try to prevent her from being hit by the traffic. This is not the manner by which I would have removed her from a classroom if her behaviour had warranted it. Physical intervention is a big grey area, not a black-and-white area. There are times when I have held a child and wished I hadn't, and there have been times when I chose not to hold and wished I had. I feel intense pressure when I have to make a decision on whether to use an RPI or not. Sometimes I have had only several seconds to decide and then had to keep thinking through my decision: *Had I done the best thing?* There is nothing pleasurable in this process. In fact, it is always the same – difficult, challenging and worrying. I do feel a certain scorn for those organisations that bitterly oppose RPI of any kind. It must be wonderful to sit and criticise practitioners about their actions. I have met, worked with and been one of those staff members that have had to restrain children to help keep a situation under control. To be faced with a child's aggressive actions and feel your well-being is under attack feels horrible and scary.

I have been fortunate that the managers and head teachers I have worked for have supported my decisions and shown respect to me for making tough decisions. Looking back, perhaps I have been lucky that they understood the thought processes that went into the decision making. How it leaves a person feeling vulnerable and scared, open to others' interpretation – days or weeks later still contemplating: *Did I do the right thing? Am I about to find myself in trouble? What will the parents think or say?*

Yes, it's difficult and I feel resentment towards the child for placing me in that situation. It is not always fair. RPI usually happens for sound reasons and we try our very best and act in good faith. Would I do the same again? Yes, I would do the same again *mostly* (I would like to think I could cut out some of my mistakes) because I'm passionate about keeping adults and children safe. I know using RPI as a last resort has helped to support numerous children retain their placement in a setting. It has prevented children from harming themselves and has avoided injuries to adults and other children. Knowing what I know now compared with 17 years ago when I first started in this profession, I would feel more confident in my practice and implement safer, better techniques. Training courses that teach RPI should be ever evolving. Course content needs to be re-evaluated and RPI techniques re-examined to ascertain if improvements could be made.

> *The best way to look as deeply as possible into the value of RPIs is to view it from the eyes of the children.*
>
> – Steve Brown

The acid test of any setting is to ask the children and young people how staff keep them safe. In every setting I have worked in and been a visitor to (as part of an outreach team), my priority has been the safety of the children that access that particular provision. I have four children between 2 and 9 years old. As much as I love them and feel the need to keep them safe, I cannot accomplish this 100 per cent. This is because they are not always with me and spend time with others. Have you ever wondered why we place a greater emphasis on the safety of other people's children than our own? I have a much greater fear of a friend's child being harmed on my watch than my own child. In fact, I have to admit that my four sons are probably more likely to succumb to accidents and injuries with me than with anyone else. I once spent two consecutive days in two different hospitals with two of my children injured under my supervision. Then a few weeks later, my third son had a seizure because of a high temperature and went to a third hospital. My fourth son spent a few sleepless nights wondering when he and his dad were going to spend some quality time together (courtesy of the British National Health Service – I got my tax monies worth that month!).

I feel parents, governing bodies, inspection teams and the media need to canvass children in school and find out what they think and how they feel they are being kept safe. We will know things are right on track if, when asked, children state any of the following:

- 'Staff keep us safe by providing places we can go to and relax.'

- 'Staff talk and listen.'

- 'The adults pre-warn us about the dangers.'

- 'The adults treat us like their own kids.'

- 'The adults hold us sometimes to keep us safe – it doesn't hurt.'

I have worked in settings where children have communicated the opposite:

- 'Staff shout at us and blame us.'

- 'The adults hurt us when they hold.'

- 'I feel they don't like me.'

- 'Staff seem disinterested.'

This is important information because it evaluates the practice of staff. Children with ASD will be especially honest and brutal in their appraisal. They need to know where they stand in terms of the reaction and approach of the staff.

Isn't it about time that the topic of using physical intervention be discussed openly and that there be an acknowledgement worldwide that there is a profound value and need to use RPI to help children stay as safe as possible?

◇◇◇

KEY POINTS

- Train all staff in the setting. Buy into an accredited training provider, if possible.

- Choose a course that promotes de-escalation as the main thrust and RPI as the last resort.

- Provide safe furniture and areas to reduce risk or hold children when it is in their best interest.

- Always exhaust all non-physical interventions before using an RPI.

- When using an RPI keep on de-escalating.

◇◇◇

Risk Assessment

Team-Teach: Risk/restraint reduction plan

www.Team-Teach.co.uk

Name: Setting:

Trigger behaviours: (Describe common behaviours or situations which are known to have led to positive handling being required. When is such behaviour likely to occur?)

'Topography' of behaviour: (Describe what the behaviour looks and/or sounds like.)

Preferred supportive and intervention strategies: (Other ways of C.A.L.M.ing such behaviours. Describe strategies that, where and when possible, should be attempted before handling techniques are used.)

Verbal advice and support	☐	Distraction (known key words, objects, likes, etc.)	☐
Reassurance	☐	Take-up time	☐
C.A.L.M talking/stance	☐	Time out (requires a written plan)	☐
Negotiation	☐	Withdrawal (requires staff or carer observation)	☐
Choices/limits	☐	Cool off: directed / offered (delete as appropriate); time allowed out to calm	☐

Humour   ☐   Contingent touch   ☐
Consequences   ☐   Transfer adult (help protocol) ☐
Planned ignoring   ☐   Success reminder   ☐
Others   ☐

Praise points or strengths (areas that can be developed and built upon):

Please list at least three bridge builders:

1.

2.

3.

Medical conditions that should be taken into account before physically intervening (e.g. asthma, brittle bones):

Preferred handling strategies: (Describe the preferred holds: standing, sitting, ground, stating numbers of staff, what "get outs" that can be used when holding, etc.)

Debriefing process following incident: (What is the care to be provided?)

Recording and notifications required:

Please print: Please sign:

Establishment: Name:

Placing authority: Name:

Parents/guardians: Name:

Name: Signature:

Date: ___ / ___ / _____   Review date: ___ / ___ / _____

Other factors to consider:

- Key behavioural difficulties

- Our understanding of the behaviour

- What we want to see instead

- Environmental changes that might help

- How the individual can help

- How parents or carers can help

- Rewarding progress

- Monitoring progress

Registered Limited Company 03770582 Director: G. Matthews Secretary: DJ Matthews
Tel: 01403 268928 / 0772 01 06 522

REFERENCES

Alexander, K.W. and Alexander, K. (2011) *Higher Education Law: Policy and Perspectives*. New York, NY: Routledge.

Allen, B. (2003) *Changing Minds: The Psychology and Philosophy of Managing Challenging Behaviour*. Redhills, UK: Steaming Publishing.

Allen, D. (2001) *Training Carers in Physical interventions: Research towards Evidence-based Practice*. Plymouth: BILD Publications.

American Psychiatric Association (APA) (2013): *Diagnostic and Statistical Manual of Mental Disorders, Fifth Edition (DSM-V)*, Arlington, VA: American Psychiatric Association.

Anderson, C. (2012) *IAN Research Report: Bullying and Children with ASD*. Baltimore, MD: Kennedy Krieger Institute. Available at www.iancommunity.org/cs/ian_research_reports/ian_research_report_bullying, accessed November 3 2014.

Anti-Bullying Alliance (2013). *Bullying and Autistic Spectrum Disorders: Guidance for Teachers and other Professionals*. London, UK: Anti-Bullying Alliance. Available at www.anti-bullyingalliance.org.uk/media/5397/ASDs-and-bulltubg-module-FINAL.pdf, accessed November 10 2014.

Borg, J. (2011) *Body Language: How to Know What's REALLY Being Said,* Second edition. Harlow: Pearson Education Ltd.

The British Institute of Learning Difficulties (BILD) (2010) *Code of Practice for the Use and Reduction of Restrictive Physical Interventions. A Guide for Trainers and Commissioners of Training*, Third edition. Birmingham, UK: BILD Publishers.

Brown, S. (2012) 'Does Team Teach Training help Autism outreach staff feel safer when supporting children with challenging behavior?', *Good Autism Practice (GAP) 13*, 1, 49.

Clements, J. and Zarkowska, E. (2000) *Behavioural Concerns and Autistic Spectrum Disorders: Explanations and Strategies for Change*. London, UK: Jessica Kingsley Publishers.

Department for Education (2010) *Restraining Pupils and Use of Force*. Available at www.education.gov.uk/schools/restraining-pupils-and-use-of-force, accessed October 10 2010.

Department for Education and Department of Health (2014) *Special Education Needs and Disability Code of Practice – 0 to 25 years: Government response* (DFE-00205-2013). Available at https://www.gov.uk/government/consultations/special-educational-needs-sen-code-of-practice-and-regulations, accessed August 29 2014.

Department of Health (1989), *The Children Act*. London, UK: The Stationery Office.

Emerson, E. (2002) 'The prevalence of use of reactive management strategies in community-based services in the UK.' In Allen, D. *Ethical Approaches to Physical Interventions: Responding to Challenging Behaviour in People with Intellectual Disabilities.* Birmingham, UK: BILD Publications.

Emerson, E., Kiernan, C., Alborz, A., Reeves, D., Mason, H., Swarbrick, R., Mason, L. and Hatton, C. (2001) 'The prevalence of challenging behaviours: A total population study.' *Research in Development Disabilities 22,* 77–93.

Field, T. (1999) 'American adolescents touch each other less and are more aggressive toward their peers as compared with French adolescents.' *Adolescence 34,* 136, 753–758.

Frith, U. (1989) *Autism: Explaining the Enigma.* London, UK: Blackwell.

Government of South Australia, Department of Education and Children's Services (2011) *Protective Practices for Staff in their Interactions with Children and Young People: Guidelines for Staff Working or Volunteering in Education and Care Settings.* Department of Education and Children's Services, Catholic Education South Australia, Association of Independent Schools of South Australia.

Grandin, T. (1996) Autism Research Institute Interview with Dr Temple Grandin conducted by Dr Stephen Edelson. Available at www.autism.com/advocacy_grandin_interview, accessed July 27 2014.

Grandin, T. (2006) *Thinking in Pictures, Expanded Edition: My Life with Autism.* New York, NY: Vintage Books.

Guerrero, L., Anderson, P. and Afifi, W. (2014) *Close Encounters: Communication in Relationships, Fourth Edition.* Thousand Oaks, CA: Sage Publishers. Available at www.psychologytoday.com/articles/201302/the-power-touch, accessed September 10 2014.

Health and Safety Executive (2004) *Manual Handling Operations Regulations 1992,* Third edition. Norwich, UK: The Stationary Office.

Jackson, L. (2002) *Freaks, Geeks and Asperger Syndrome: A User's Guide to Adolescence.* London, UK: Jessica Kingsley Publishers.

Kanner, L (1943) 'Autistic disturbances of affective contact.' *Nervous Child 2,* 217–250.

Kemp, E. and Merkelbach, M. (2011) 'Can you get sued?' *Security Management Initiative, Policy Paper.* Geneva, Switzerland: Security Management Initiative.

Knight, S. (2009) *NLP at Work: The Essence of Excellence,* Third edition. London, UK: Nicholas Brearley Publishing.

Leadbetter, D. (2002) 'Good practice in physical interventions.' In Allen, D. (2002) *Ethical Approaches to Physical Interventions: Responding to Challenging Behaviour in People with Intellectual Disabilities.* Birmingham, UK: BILD Publications.

Mitchell, D. and Higashida, N. (2013) *The Reason I Jump.* London, UK: Hodder and Stoughton.

Paron-Wildes, A.J. (2008) 'Sensory stimulation and Autistic children.' *Implications 6,* 4. University of Minnesota. Available at www.informedesign.org/_news/apr_v06r-pr.pdf, accessed August 2 2014.

Ogburn, C. (1957) 'Merrill's Marauders.' *Harper's Magazine 2214,* 1280, 32–33.

Pellicano, L., Dinsmore, A. and Charman, T. (2013) *A Future Made Together: Shaping Autism Research in the UK.* London, UK: Centre For Research in Autism and Education (CRAE).

Rickford, F. 'Assault part of the job?' *Learning Support Magazine, 2,* 33. (2010) Bishop's Castle, UK: Brightday Publishing.

Robers, S., Kemp, J., Rathbun, A., and Morgan, R.E. (2014). *Indicators of School Crime and Safety: 2013* (NCES 2014-042/NCJ 243299). Washington, DC: National Center for Education Statistics, U.S. Department of Education, and Bureau of Justice Statistics, Office of Justice Programs, U.S. Department of Justice.

Sanderson, H. and Harrison, J. (1991) *Aromatherapy and Massage for People with Learning Difficulties.* Birmingham, UK: Hands on Publishing.

Schultz, J. (2012) *Eye Contact: An Introduction to its role in Communication.* Michigan State University Extension. Available at http://mseu.anr.msu.edu/news/eye_contact_an_introduction_to_its_role_in_communication, accessed July 21 2014.

Sperling, G. (1963) 'A model for visual memory tasks.' *Human Factors 5*, 19–31.

State of New Mexico Public Education Department (2006) *Use of Physical Restraint as a Behavioural Intervention for Students with Disabilities.* Available at www.ped.state.nm.us/SEB/law/Restraint.Policy.pdf, accessed July 24 2014.

Tulving, E. (1972) 'Episodic and semantic memory.' In Tulving, E. and Donaldson, W. (eds) *Organisation of Memory.* New York, NY: New York Academic Press.

US Department of Education (2009) *Key Policy Letters Signed by the Education Secretary or Deputy Secretary, Arne Duncan.* Washington, DC: Department of Education.

United States Senate Health, Education, Labor and Pensions Committee (Tom Harkin, Chairman) (2014) *Dangerous Use of Seclusion and Restraints in Schools Remains Widespread and Difficult to Remedy: A review of Ten Cases. Majority Committee Staff Report.* Available at www.help.senate.gov/imo/media/doc/Seclusion%20and%20Restraints%20Final%20Report.pdf, accessed 11 November 2014.

Vasagar, Jeevan (2011) 'Michael Gove slackens rules on use of physical force in schools.' *The Guardian.* Available at www.theguardian.com/politics/2011/sep/01/michael-gove-physical-force-schools, accessed 11 November 2014.

Wheldall, K., Bevan, K. and Shortall, K. (1986) 'A touch of reinforcement: The effects of contingent touch on the classroom behaviour of young children.' *Educational Review 38*, 207–216.

Wolfendale, S. and Robinson, M. (2006) 'Meeting Special Needs in the Early Years: An Inclusive Stance.' In Pugh, G. and Duffy, B. (eds) *Contemporary Issues in the Early Years.* Fourth edition. London, UK: Sage Publications.

INDEX

Printed in Great Britain
by Amazon